全球重要农业文化遗产保护的中国经验
China's Experience in the Conservation of Globally Important Agricultural Heritage Systems (GIAHS)

内蒙古敖汉旱作农业系统保护与发展实践

Conservation and Development Practices in Aohan Dryland Farming System of Inner Mongolia Autonomous Region

焦雯珺　孙业红　徐　峰　编著
Written by JIAO Wenjun, SUN Yehong and XU Feng

中国农业科学技术出版社
China Agricultural Science and Technology Press

图书在版编目（CIP）数据

内蒙古敖汉旱作农业系统保护与发展实践 / 焦雯珺，孙业红，徐峰编著 .— 北京：中国农业科学技术出版社，2020.8

ISBN 978-7-5116-4920-1

Ⅰ . ①内… Ⅱ . ①焦… ②孙… ③徐… Ⅲ . ①旱作农业—文化遗产—保护—研究—敖汉旗②旱作农业—农业经济—经济发展—研究—敖汉旗 Ⅳ . ① F327.264

中国版本图书馆 CIP 数据核字（2020）第 144265 号

责任编辑 穆玉红
责任校对 李向荣

出 版 者 中国农业科学技术出版社
北京市中关村南大街 12 号 邮编：100081
电 话 （010）82109707 82106626（编辑室）（010）82109702（发行部）
（010）82109709（读者服务部）
传 真 （010）82106626
网 址 http://www.castp.cn
发 行 各地新华书店
印 刷 者 北京富泰印刷有限责任公司
开 本 787 mm × 1 092 mm 1 /16
印 张 12.5
字 数 380 千字
版 次 2020 年 8 月第 1 版 2020 年 8 月第 1 次印刷
定 价 88.00 元

策　　划： 中国科学院地理科学与资源研究所自然与文化遗产研究中心

内蒙古自治区赤峰市敖汉旗人民政府

Planned by: Center for Natural and Cultural Heritage, Institute of Geographic Sciences and Natural Resources Research, Chinese Academy of Sciences

People's Government of Aohan Banner, Chifeng City, Inner Mongolia Autonomous Region

支　　持： 农业农村部国际合作司

农业农村部农村社会事业促进司

中国农学会农业文化遗产分会

Supported by: Department of International Cooperation, Ministry of Agriculture and Rural Affairs, P. R. China

Department of Rural Social Services, Ministry of Agriculture and Rural Affairs, P. R. China

Agricultural Heritage Branch of China Association of Agricultural Science Societies

顾　　问： 李文华　闵庆文　邱文博　于宝君　赵常山

主　　编： 焦雯珺　孙业红　徐　峰

参编人员（按姓氏笔画排列）：

史媛媛　刘显洋　武文杰　姚灿灿　索良喜　崔文超

Consultants: LI Wenhua　MIN Qingwen　QIU Wenbo　YU Baojun　ZHAO Changshan

Main Authors: JIAO Wenjun　SUN Yehong　XU Feng

Participants (orderded by strokes of family names):

SHI Yuanyuan　LIU Xianyang　WU Wenjie　YAO Cancan　SUO Liangxi　CUI Wenchao

探索农业文化遗产保护的“敖汉模式”

居家抗“疫”期间，很高兴收到焦雯珺副研究员发来的《内蒙古敖汉旱作农业系统保护与发展实践》书稿，并被邀请为之作“序”。虽感勉为其难，但为表示对这项工作的支持，还是答应了。当然还有另外的原因，就是想借此机会梳理一下和敖汉的“缘分”，表达一下对敖汉旗在农业文化遗产保护工作中所付出艰辛努力和取得显著成效的敬佩，也顺便表达一下我对农业文化遗产保护工作的想法。

严格说来，这不是一部学术性很强的论著，但确是一部值得推荐的农业文化遗产保护的参考书，因为“敖汉旱作农业系统”是我国全球重要农业文化遗产（GIAHS）保护较为成功的案例之一。

我最早知道“敖汉旱作农业文化”是通过一位来自内蒙古自治区（全书简称内蒙古）的同事。大概是在 2009 年，他知道我在做联合国粮食及农业组织（FAO）牵头的全球环境基金（GEF）多国项目“GIAHS 动态保护与适应性管理”，就告诉我“内蒙古自治区赤峰市的敖汉旗是一个值得关注的地方，那里不仅有史前文化、玉龙文化，还有旱作农业文化”。因为他是研究地理信息系统的，对于相关农业文化方面能提供的资料有限，加上我当时正忙于浙江青田、贵州从江、江西万年等地的工作，也无暇顾及，就

没太在意。

之后是在 2010 年年底，我非常敬重的一位学者，也是对我工作给予极大支持的众多学者之一的中国社会科学院考古研究所的植物考古与农业考古专家赵志军先生（他在江西万年仙人洞遗址的稻作起源考古研究和内蒙古敖汉兴隆洼遗址的旱作起源考古研究堪称经典，而且也是这两个地方申报 GIAHS 的重要技术支撑），在电话中告诉我敖汉旗领导有意申报 GIAHS 保护试点（当时是 GEF 项目执行期，所以申报的项目都称为"保护试点"），我当即允诺将全力支持。随后就有了 2011 年 3 月在北京召开的"农业文化遗产地农产品开发与管理研讨会"上与时任敖汉旗副旗长邢和平先生就申遗工作进行的交流，和 7 月第一次带领团队去敖汉的实地考察。

多次到敖汉，虽每次时间都不长，但很多人、很多事都给我留下了深刻印象：第一次入住敖汉旗政府招待所，就发现了旁边竖立的一个写着"全球重要农业文化遗产主要候选地敖汉旗欢迎您"的十分醒目的宣传牌，记得邢和平副旗长跟我说，"我们就是想让全旗干部群众和到旗里来的客人都知道我们在做的这件事"；几次在敖汉旗关于 GIAHS 申报和保护的座谈会、报告会上，旗委、政府、人大、政协主要领导全员出席，邱文博书记跟我说，"四大班子主要领导全员出席说明了这件事在我们旗里工作的重要地位"；在 2012 年 3 月北京"中华农耕文化展"上，时任旗长黄彦峰亲自向参观者介绍敖汉历史文化和旱作农业系统的保护与发展情况；连续举办"世界小米起源大会"，邱文博书记、于宝君旗长每次都充满自豪地宣介敖汉小米和敖汉文化。不仅是这些领导、这些事，还有通过 GIAHS 保护结识的长期痴迷于农业文化遗产保护工作、被誉为"一片忠情传谷香"的旗农牧业局高级农艺师徐峰，借助 GIAHS 品牌不断拓展小米产业、带领农民脱贫致富的合作社社长王国军，不断创新农业文化遗产保护理念、堪称"新农人"代表的返乡创业大学生刘海庆等"小人物"，以及作为"中国重要农业文化遗产系列读本"之一的图书《内蒙古敖汉旱作农业系统》，第一版发行即售罄而加印，"敖汉小米，熬出中国味"成功登陆央视，使敖汉小米成为央视上榜品牌和"一县一品"扶贫品牌，等等。

当然，还有一件事令我颇感意外但一直引以为自豪。2016 年 9 月我获得了敖汉旗委、政府颁发的一个"荣誉证书"——"闵庆文研究员：您为敖汉小米产业发展做出突出贡献，荣获先进个人奖"。这是我参加工作后获得的颁奖单位"级别最低"的奖励，但却一直被我视为"级别最高"的荣誉。

也正是因为这些原因，我对敖汉旗的领导和群众一直心怀敬佩与感激，也对敖汉的农业文化遗产保护工作充满着希冀与期盼。期待着他们在农业文化遗产保护中不断探索、不断创新，正如收入本书的我的一篇短文最后所说："祝愿'敖汉小米甲天下'成为现实，祝愿敖汉旱作农业系统这一世界上第一个也是目前唯一一个以传统旱作为主体的全球重要农业文化遗产保护好、传承好、利用好，成为世界农业文化遗产保护与发展的样板。"

可以说，我的期待与祝愿已经成为现实。一个直接的证明就是，敖汉旱作农业系统不仅得到了很好的保护和传承，而且成功助推了以“敖汉小米”为代表的旱作农业产业的快速发展，不仅与文化、旅游等相关产业相得益彰，更在敖汉成功推出“国家扶贫开发工作重点县”的过程中发挥了重要作用。具体的做法与成效，本书作了较为全面的介绍，这里不再赘述。我认为，称为“农业文化遗产保护的敖汉模式”，实不为过。

从敖汉的工作，我想到了全球重要农业文化遗产的保护问题。

我自 2005 年在导师李文华院士的引领下，参与了 FAO 牵头的 GEF 项目的申请与执行，参与了中国几乎全部 GIAHS 项目的申请，到过全世界目前 59 个 GIAHS 项目中的 37 个（包括中国的全部 15 个项目的所有点，菲律宾、日本、韩国、伊朗、斯里兰卡、肯尼亚、墨西哥、意大利 8 个国家的 22 个项目点），曾担任 FAO GIAHS 项目科学委员会委员、现仍任 FAO GIAHS 科学咨询小组共同主席，可以说是 GIAHS 工作的亲眼见证者和全程参与者。更多时候是为所取得的成就而兴奋并对未来的发展充满信心，但又时常会因所面临的问题而掠过一些不安。这些问题中，较为突出的是领导重视不够、社会认知度不高、学科之间与部门之间缺乏有效合作，等等。

15 年的工作，使我越来越我认识到：GIAHS 发掘与保护是一个跨学科的全新领域，需要多学科的科研人员共同参与；GIAHS 发掘与保护是一项跨部门的综合工作，需要多部门的管理人员共同努力；GIAHS 保护成功与否的关键，是其“创造者”（农民）是否愿意继续在其“栖息地”（农村）从事产生其所有功能与价值的最主要活动（农业）。一句话，GIAHS 不是一般意义上的文化遗产，也不是一般意义上的农业生产，需要探索新的保护机制与模式。

农业文化遗产的保护形势不容乐观，位于菲律宾伊富高省内的科迪勒拉水稻梯田于 1995 年被联合国教科文组织（UNESCO）列入世界文化遗产，成为亚洲第一个被列入该名录的农业类型的文化景观，很快享誉全球，但由于传统品种减少、外来物种入侵、旅游发展过度、梯田面积缩减等多种原因，2001 年被世界遗产委员会列入世界濒危遗产名单。

有意思的是，菲律宾伊富高梯田不仅是世界文化遗产，而且还于 2005 年被 FAO 列为首批 GIAHS 保护试点。无独有偶，我国云南红河哈尼梯田先后于 2010 年、2013 年分别被 FAO、UNESCO 列为 GIAHS 保护试点和世界文化遗产。

关于 GIAHS 保护工作，常可以听到这样两种说法：一种是，自 FAO 于 2002 年发起 GIAHS 保护倡议以来只有 18 年，在各方努力之下，目前已有 22 个国家的 59 个项目被列入 GIAHS 名录，还有一批申报项目在评审中，特别是在 2015 年联合国大会后 GIAHS 工作被列入常规预算。GIAHS 及其保护已经取得较为广泛的共识。

另一种说法是，自 FAO 于 2002 年发起 GIAHS 保护倡议以来已有 18 年，虽经各方努力，目前只有 22 个国家的 59 个项目被列入 GIAHS 名录。无论其数量还是社会认可度，都远远不能与联合国教科文组织（UNESCO）的世界遗产（截至 2019 年年底共有 1 121 项，分布在 167 个国家）相比。

两种说法都对。第一种说法固然让人振奋，但第二种说法确实也让我们认真思考一些问题，比如：如何更好地解读 GIAHS 的概念与内涵才能让更多的人关注并了解？如何通过 GIAHS 品牌效应的更好发挥从而促进其保护？如何更好发挥 GIAHS 在脱贫攻坚、美丽中国建设和乡村振兴战略中的作用而使其潜在价值得到更大程度释放……

问题很多，"探索"永远在路上。我曾经提出，对于农业文化遗产这一特殊的遗产类型，其保护应当建立"三个关键机制"：以生态与文化保护补偿为核心的"政策激励机制"；以农业生产、功能拓展、融合发展为特征的的"产业促进机制"；由政府、科技、企业、农民、社会构成的"五位一体"的"多方参与机制"。

这只是理论上的思考，尚需要实践上的验证。敖汉的实践可否作为一个验证呢？还请读者明辨。

是为序。

2020 年 5 月 8 日

Exploring the "Aohan Model" of the Conservation of the Agricultural Heritage System

During the "social distancing" period at home, I was very glad to receive the manuscripts of *Conservation and Development Practices in Aohan Dryland Farming System of Inner Mongolia Autonomous Region* sent by Associate Professor Jiao Wenjun and was invited to preface the book. At first I was a bit reluctant; however, I agreed to show my support for this work. There were also other reasons. I wanted to take this opportunity to sort out my "ties" with Aohan, express my admiration for arduous efforts and remarkable achievements of Aohan Banner in their conservation work of the agricultural heritage system and also passingly share my ideas on the conservation of agricultural heritage systems.

Strictly speaking, this is not a strong academic works but indeed a recommendable reference book on the conservation of agricultural heritage systems, for "Aohan Dryland Farming System" is one of the more successful cases on the conservation of the Globally Important Agricultural Heritage Systems (GIAHS) in our country.

I knew "Aohan" first from a colleague from Inner Mongolia. Around 2009, when he learned that I was engaged in a GEF project titled "Dynamic Conservation and Adaptive Management of Globally Important Agricultural Heritage Systems (GIAHS)" led by the Food and Agriculture Organization (FAO), he told me that Aohan Banner in Chifeng City, Inner Mongolia Autonomous Region was a noteworthy place where there were not only prehistoric culture, Yulong culture, but also dryland farming culture. Since he was a research fellow of geographic information system, he could not told me more about it; I was then busily engaged in my work in Qingtian of Zhejiang Province, Congjiang of Guizhou Province and Wannian of Jiangxi Province, so I did not have time for it, thus not taking it to heart.

Later, at the end of 2010, Mr. Zhao Zhijun, a highly respected scholar and one of those scholars giving great support to my work, an expert in plant and agricultural archaeology in the Institute of Archaeology, Chinese Academy of Social Sciences (whose archaeological research on the origins of rice at the Xianrendong Cave in Wannian of Jiangxi Province and the origins of dryland farming at the Xinglongwa Site in Aohan of Inner Mongolia could be rated as classic, thus becoming the major technical support for these two places to apply for GIAHS) told me on the phone that the leaders of Aohan Banner intended to apply for GIAHS pilots (at that time, it was the execution period of GEF project, so the designated projects were all referred to as "pilots"). I immediately promised to give my all-out support. Soon afterwards, I had exchanges with Mr. Xing Heping, then deputy head of Aohan Banner regarding the application work for GIAHS at the “Seminar on Agricultural Products Development and Management in Agricultural Heritage Sites” held in Beijing in March, 2011 and in July for the first time, I led the team and had a field survey in Aohan.

Time after time I went to Aohan and I was deeply impressed by many people and things there though every time I did not stay long. When I first checked in the government hostel of Aohan Banner, I found an eye-catching billboard erected next to the hostel which read "Welcome to Aohan Banner, a major candidate to Globally Important Agricultural Heritage Systems". What the Deputy Head Xing Heping told me called to mind: "We just want the cadres and the masses in Aohan Banner and all the visitors to know what we are doing right now". And for several times all of the main leaders from the Banner party committee, the Banner government, the NPC and the CPPCC attended the forums and seminars on GIAHS application and conservation held in Aohan Banner. Qiu Wenbo, secretary of the Banner party committee, told me that, "The full attendance of four major leaderships illustrates the important role it has in Aohan Banner." In the "Chinese Farming Culture Exhibition" held in March, 2013, Mr. Huang Yanfeng, the then head of Aohan Banner, introduced to visitors in person about the history and culture of Aohan and the conservation and development of dryland farming system. The "International Conference of Millet" was held continuously, and each time Secretary Qiu Wenbo and Head Yu Baojun would introduce Aohan millet and Aohan culture proudly.... Apart from these leaders and things, during my GIAHS conservation work I also got to know senior agronomist Xu Feng from Agriculture and Animal Husbandry Bureau of Aohan Banner who had long been obsessed with the conservation of the agricultural heritage system and was honored as "a loyal lover to pass on grain fragrance", Wang Guojun, the director-general of the cooperative who made use of GIAHS brand to constantly expand millet industry and lead farmers to cast off poverty and set out on a road to prosperity, Liu Haiqing, a college student who returned to his hometown to start a business, constantly innovated the concept of agricultural heritage conservation and could be called as the representative of "New Farmers", and other "nobodies". I also witnessed "Aohan Dryland Farming System of Inner Mongolia Autonomous Region", one of the "China Nationally Important Agricultural Heritage Systems Series Books" becoming the first volume sold out for the first print and the only overprinted edition, as well as the Aohan millet that successfully landed on CCTV program with the advertising slogan “Having Aohan Millet, Tasting Chinese Flavor”and thus became a listed brand of CCTV National Brand Plan and the poverty alleviation brand of “One County, One Speciality”, and the like.

Of course, there was another thing that surprised me and I took pride in at all times. In September 2016, I received an honorary certificate issued from Aohan Banner party committee and government, which read "Professor Min Qingwen wins the Advanced Individual Award for his outstanding contributions to the development of Aohan millet industry". This was the award with the lowest level of awarding unit among those I received after I began to work, but with the honor of the highest level I had always regarded as.

For these reasons, I have always admired and appreciated the leaders and the masses in Aohan Banner and always had hopes and expectations for the conservation work of the agricultural heritage system in Aohan. I have been looking forward to their continuous exploration and innovations in their conservation work of the agricultural heritage system. Just like my essay included in this book said in conclusion: "I wish that "Aohan Millet is the best in the world" will come true and hope the Aohan Dryland Farming System, the world's first and currently the only GIAHS with traditional dryland farming as its main body, will be well conserved, inherited and utilized and become the model for the conservation and development of agricultural heritage systems in the world."

Now, I can say that my expectations and wishes have come true. There is a direct proof that Aohan Dryland Farming System not only has been well protected and inherited, but also has successfully promoted the rapid development of the dryland farming industry represented by "Aohan millet", which not only complements the culture, tourism and other related industries, but also plays an important role in the successful launch of "Key Counties of the

State's Poverty Alleviation and Development Work" in Aohan. This book has a comprehensive introduction to the specific approaches and effects, which will not be detailed here. I think it is nothing exaggerating to be regarded as "the Aohan model of the Agricultural Heritage Conservation".

From the conservation work in Aohan, I thought of the conservation issues about GIAHS.

Since 2005, I have participated in the application and implementation of the GEF project led by the FAO under the guidance of my tutor, Academician Li Wenhua and participated in the application of almost all GIAHS projects in China. I have been to 37 of the 59 GIAHS projects in the world (including all the sites under 15 projects of China, and 22 projects in 8 countries like Philippines, Japan, South Korea, Iran, Sri Lanka, Kenya, Mexico, Italy and so on). I once served as the member of the FAO GIAHS Science Committee and now the Co-chairman of the FAO GIAHS Scientific Advisory Group. So I dare say I am the full participant and eyewitness of GIAHS work. Most of the time I was excited for these achievements and confident about the future; but every now and then I was a bit concerned about the problems I met. Among these problems, there were more prominent ones like not enough attention from leadership, low social awareness, the lack of effective cooperation between departments and between disciplines, and so on.

After 15 years of work, I come to realize that the GIAHS exploration and conservation is a brand-new interdisciplinary field that needs joint participation of multidisciplinary researchers; the GIAHS exploration and conservation is a cross-department comprehensive work that requires joint efforts of managerial staff from many departments; the key to the success of GIAHS conservation is whether the "creators" (farmers) are willing to continue their major work (agriculture) that produces all functions and values in their "habitats" (villages). In a word, GIAHS is not a cultural heritage or agricultural production in a general sense. New conservation mechanisms and models need to be explored.

There are not many successful cases but still some lessons to learn. The Cordillera rice terraces in Ifugao Province of the Philippines were listed in the World Cultural Heritage by the United Nations Educational Scientific and Cultural Organization (UNESCO) in 1995, and became the first agricultural landscape in Asia to be listed and soon gained global reputation. However, due to reduction of traditional varieties, invasion of alien species, excessive tourism development, reduction of terraces area and other reasons, it was listed in the List of World Endangered Heritage Sites by World Heritage Committee in 2001.

Interestingly, the Ifugao terraces of the Philippines were not only World Cultural Heritage, but also listed as the first batch of GIAHS pilots by the FAO in 2005. Coincidentally, the Honghe Hani rice terraces in Yunnan Province were listed as a GIAHS pilot and World Cultural Heritage by the FAO and UNESCO respectively in 2010 and 2013.

We can often hear two statements regarding the conservation work of GIAHS: one is that there has been only 18 years since the FAO launched the GIAHS conservation initiative in 2002. Under the efforts of all parties, at present 59 projects from 22 countries are included in the list of GIAHS, and a number of projects are under review, and the GIAHS work is in particular included in the regular budget after the 2015 UN General Assembly. The GIAHS and its conservation work have been widely recognized.

Another point of view is that it has been 18 years since the FAO launched the GIAHS conservation initiative in 2002. Despite the efforts of all parties, only 59 projects from 22 countries have been listed in the GIAHS list. No matter the amount or social acceptance, it is far beyond comparison to the UNESCO's World Heritage (there were 1121 projects in 167 countries by the end of 2019).

Both are right. The first one is no doubt exciting; but the second one really makes us to think about some problems, such as: how can we better interpret the concept and connotation of the GIAHS so that more people can pay close attention to and understand it? How can we promote the GIAHS conservation through better performance of GIAHS brand effects? How can we give full play to the role of GIAHS in the poverty alleviation, construction of beautiful China and rural revitalization strategies so as to release its potential value to a greater extent...

There are many problems, and we are always on the way of "exploration". I once proposed that for the agricultural heritage system, a special heritage type, its conservation work should establish "three key mechanisms": the "policy incentive mechanism" with compensation for ecological and cultural conservation as the core, the "industrial promotion mechanism" featured in agricultural production, function expansion and integrated development, and the "5-in-1 multi-stakeholder participation mechanism" constituted by government, technology, enterprises, farmers and society.

This is only a theoretical thinking that still needs to be verified in practice. I invite the readers to discern whether the Aohan practices could be used as a testimony.

This serves the preface.

May 8, 2020

前 言

为了保护具有全球重要性的传统农业系统，联合国粮食及农业组织于 2002 年发起全球重要农业文化遗产（GIAHS）保护倡议。2012 年，以粟和黍的种植为代表的敖汉旱作农业系统被认定为全球重要农业文化遗产，成为全球第一个旱作农业文化遗产。为加强我国重要农业文化遗产的挖掘、保护、传承和利用，原农业部（现农业农村部）于 2012 年开始中国重要农业文化遗产（China-NIAHS）发掘与保护工作。2013 年，内蒙古敖汉旱作农业系统被列为首批中国重要农业文化遗产（China-NIAHS）。

自获得认定以来，敖汉旗坚持“在保护中发展，在发展中保护”的原则，积极探索敖汉旱作农业系统保护与发展的方法与路径。在遗产的保护与传承上，敖汉旗积极开展传统品种的搜集、整理、保护与利用，开展优秀农耕文化宣传普及活动，设立专门资金支持建设敖汉旗旱作农业展览馆。在遗产的发展与利用上，敖汉旗大力建设优质谷子生产基地，加强绿色和有机生产，把敖汉小米培育成全国著名的区域公用品牌；开发微电影、儿童绘本等文化产品，打造特色旅游品牌，将农业、文化和旅游进行产业融合发展。在遗产地能力建设上，敖汉旗通过多元途径开展宣传推广工作，连续举办六届世界小米大会；实施创新人才孵化计划，鼓励农村青年返乡创业；培育龙头企业和农民合作社，带动贫困户增收脱贫。经过多年的积极探索，敖汉旗成为中国北方地区农业文化遗产保护的先行者，演绎了“小米撬动世界，遗产大有可为”的佳话。

本书将有助于读者了解敖汉旗为保护与发展敖汉旱作农业系统所开展的实践探索以及在实践过程中所积累的宝贵经验，也有助于提高全社会对重要农业文化遗产及其价值的认识和保护意识。全书正文包括四篇共 17 章："第一篇 遗产价值解读" 由 3 章构成，分别介绍了敖汉旱作农业系统的特征与价值、整个申遗过程以及专家对敖汉旱作农业系统的理解；"第二篇 遗产保护与传承" 由 4 章构成，分别介绍了在敖汉旗开展的考古工作及考古价值挖掘、敖汉旗开展的传统品种收集与整理工作、传统知识和传统文化的保护与传承工作；"第三篇 遗产发展与利用" 由 5 章构成，分别介绍了敖汉旗开展的种质资源研究与利用工作、文化产品与可持续旅游开发工作、敖汉旗具有代表性的农民专业合作社和龙头企业的情况；"第四篇 遗产地能力建设" 由 5 章构成，分别介绍了敖汉旗开展的宣传与培训工作、敖汉旗的科技与市场合作情况、国际与区域交流情况、农村青年返乡创业情况以及通过遗产保护助力脱贫攻坚的情况。"附录" 部分提供了全球 / 中国重要农业文化遗产名录。

本书是在文献调研和实地调研的基础上编写完成的，是集体智慧的结晶。全书由焦雯珺、孙业红、徐峰设计框架并牵头编写，崔文超、武文杰、姚灿灿、刘显洋、史媛媛等参与了各章节的编写，焦雯珺、孙业红、徐峰统稿。本书在编写过程中得到了李文华院士和闵庆文研究员的具体指导、农业农村部国际合作司、农业农村部农村社会事业促进司、内蒙古自治区赤峰市敖汉旗人民政府及有关部门和乡镇的大力支持，在此一并表示感谢！

由于水平所限，难免存在不当之处，敬请读者批评指正。

编　者

2020 年 4 月 28 日

Introduction

In order to conserve traditional agricultural systems of global importance, Food and Agriculture Organization of the United Nations (FAO) initiated a global partnership on the conservation of the Globally Important Agricultural Heritage Systems (GIAHS) in 2002. Aohan Dryland Farming System, represented by the planting of the millet and the broomcorn millet, was designated as GIAHS by FAO in 2012, becoming the first dryland farming heritage in the world. To strengthen the exploration, conservation, inheritance and utilization of important agricultural heritage systems in China, the Ministry of Agriculture (current Ministry of Agriculture and Rural Affairs) of the People's Republic of China started the exploration and conservation of China Nationally Important Agricultural Heritage Systems (China-NIAHS) in 2012. Aohan Dryland Farming System was listed in the first batch of China-NIAHS by the Ministry in 2013.

Since the designation, Aohan Banner has actively explored the conservation and development methods and ways of Aohan Dryland Farming System based on the principle that "develop it through the conservation and conserve it during the development". With regard to the conservation and inheritance of the heritage, Aohan Banner has actively collected, collated, protected and utilized the traditional varieties, held the publicity activity of excellent

farming culture and established special fund to support the construction of Aohan dryland farming exhibition hall. With regard to the development and utilization of the heritage, Aohan Banner has vigorously established the production base of high-quality millet, strengthened the production of the green and organic agricultural products and cultivated Aohan millet to be famous regional public brand all over the country; Aohan Banner has also developed the relevant cultural products such as microfilms and picture books for children, built the tourism brand with local characteristics and pursued the industrial integrated development of agriculture, culture and tourism. With regard to the construction of the heritage site capacity, Aohan Banner has publicized and promoted the heritage in all forms. For example, Aohan Banner has held successive six international conferences on the millet; Aohan Banner has implemented the incubation plan of the innovative talents and encouraged rural youth to return to hometown and start a business; Aohan Banner has committed itself to cultivating leading enterprises and farmers' cooperatives to help the poverty-stricken families to increase incomes and shake off poverty. After years of active exploration, Aohan Banner has become the pioneer in northern area of China with regard to the conservation of agricultural heritage system. Aohan Banner has created a reputation that "millet can influence the world and the heritage can play an important role".

This book will not only help readers to learn about the practical exploration made by Aohan Banner to conserve and develop Aohan Dryland Farming System and the valuable experience accumulated during the practice, but also help to improve people's knowledge and conservation awareness toward the important agricultural heritage systems and their values. The whole book consists of four parts with 17 chapters: "Part Ⅰ Interpretation of the Heritage Values" is composed of 3 chapters, which introduce characteristics and values of Aohan Dryland Farming System, the whole application process for GIAHS and experts' understanding toward Aohan Dryland Farming System respectively; "Part Ⅱ Conservation and Inheritance of the Heritage System" is composed of 4 chapters, which introduce the archaeological excavation carried out in Aohan Banner and its archaeological values, the collection and collation of traditional varieties carried out by Aohan Banner, and the conservation and inheritance of traditional knowledge and traditional culture respectively; "Part Ⅲ Development and Utilization of the Heritage System" consists of 5 chapters, which introduce the study and utilization of germplasm resources carried out by Aohan Banner, the development of cultural products and sustainable tourism, the information on representative farmers' specialized cooperatives and leading enterprises in Aohan Banner respectively; "Part Ⅳ Capacity Building of the Heritage Site" consists of 5 chapters, which introduce the publicity and training work carried out by Aohan Banner, the scientific and technological cooperation and the market cooperation of Aohan Banner, the exchange of Aohan Banner with international society and other regions, the information about rural young people's returning to their hometown to start businesses and the information about the poverty alleviation by means of the heritage conservation respectively. "Appendix" provides the list of GIAHS and the list of China-NIAHS.

This book, written on the basis of the literature review and the on-site investigation, is the collective wisdom of all participants. The framework of the whole book is designed by Jiao Wenjun, Sun Yehong and Xu Feng. They also lead the writing of the whole book. Cui Wenchao, Wu Wenjie, Yao Cancan, Liu Xianyang and Shi Yuanyuan participate in the writing of specific chapters. Jian Wenjun, Sun Yehong and Xu Feng are responsible for the final compilation and edit. During the writing process, academician Li Wenhua and professor Min Qingwen have provided concrete guidance; Department of International Cooperation, Ministry of Agriculture and Rural Affairs, P. R. China, Department of Rural Social Services, Ministry of Agriculture and Rural Affairs, P. R. China, People's Government of Aohan Banner, Chifeng City, Inner Mongolia Autonomous Region and relevant bureaus as well as towns in Aohan Banner have provided vigorous support. Thanks for their help and support.

Due to the limit of our capacities, there is probably something inappropriate in this book. We are looking forward to our readers' criticism and correction.

Authors

April 28, 2020

目录

第一篇　遗产价值解读

第二篇　遗产保护与传承

第三篇　遗产发展与利用

第四篇　遗产地能力建设

附　录

Part Ⅰ Interpretation of the Heritage Values

Part Ⅱ Conservation and Inheritance of the Heritage System

Part Ⅲ Development and Utilization of the Heritage System

Part Ⅳ Capacity Building of the Heritage Site

Appendix

Interpretation of the Heritage Values

遗产价值解读

CHAPTER 1 第1章

Characteristics and Values

遗产特征与价值

敖汉旗位于内蒙古自治区赤峰市东南部，其独特的地理环境和气候条件为旱作农业的发展提供了基础。以粟[①]和黍[②]种植为代表的敖汉旱作农业系统传承数千年，于 2012 年被联合国粮食及农业组织（FAO）认定为全球重要农业文化遗产（GIAHS），成为全球第一个旱作农业文化遗产，于 2013 年被农业部（现农业农村部）列为首批中国重要农业文化遗产（China-NIAHS）。

"全球重要农业文化遗产"中文牌匾（敖汉旗农牧局 / 提供）
GIAHS Plaque in Chinese (Provided by Agriculture and Animal Husbandry Bureau of Aohan Banner (hereinafter referred to as AAHB))

"中国重要农业文化遗产"牌匾（敖汉旗农牧局 / 提供）
China-NIAHS Plaque (Provided by AAHB)

旱作农业起源地之一

敖汉旗是中国古代农业文明与草原文明的交汇处，境内分布着被誉为"华夏第一村"的兴隆洼遗址和"旱作农业发源地"之一的兴隆沟遗址。经考古证实，兴隆沟遗址发掘的碳化粟和黍距今 7 700—8 000 年，比中欧地区发现的粟早 2 700 年，是当今世界上所知较早的人工栽植形态的谷物。专家们由此推断，西辽河上游地区是粟和黍的起源地之一，是中国古代北方旱作农业的起源地之一，也是横跨欧亚大陆旱作农业的发源地之一。

① 粟，俗称谷子，一年生草本植物。籽实去壳后的产物，直径 1 毫米左右，因其粒小，得名小米 .

Millet, also named foxtail millet, is an annual herb. The fruit of millet after removing the hull is called Xiaomi in Chinese, as its diameter is about 1 millimeter only.

② 黍，俗称黍子，一年生草本植物。植株叫黍子，籽实叫黍，去壳后叫黍米，俗称大黄米 .

Broomcorn millet is an annual herb. Its plant is called Shuzi and its fruit is called Shu in Chinese. After removing the hull, the fruit of broomcorn millet is called Dahuangmi in Chinese by local people.

Aohan Banner is located in the southeast of Chifeng City, Inner Mongolia Autonomous Region. The unique geographical environment and climate conditions have laid a foundation for the development of the dryland farming in Aohan Banner. Aohan Dryland Farming System which is represented by the planting of the millet① and the broomcorn millet② has been passed down for thousands of years. It was designated as Globally Important Agricultural Heritage System (GIAHS) by Food and Agriculture Organization of the United Nations (FAO) in 2012, becoming the first dryland farming heritage in the world. Aohan Dryland Farming System was listed in the first batch of China Nationally Important Agricultural Heritage Systems (China-NIAHS) by the Ministry of Agriculture (current Ministry of Agriculture and Rural Affairs) of the People's Republic of China in 2013.

One of Origin Areas of the Dryland Farming

Aohan Banner, as an intersection between Chinese ancient agricultural civilization and the pastureland civilization, boasts both Xinglongwa Site which is honored as the "First Village of Ancient China" and Xinglonggou Site which is one of the "origin areas of the dryland farming" within its borders. The archaeological proof has verified that the millet carbide and the broomcorn millet carbide unearthed at Xinglonggou Site were 7700-8000 years ago, which is 2700 years earlier than the millet discovered in central Europe. The millet and the broomcorn millet unearthed in Aohan Banner are known as the early cereal planted by people in the world. Experts, based on the above discovery, infer that the upstream area of West Liaohe River is one of the origin areas of the millet and the broomcorn millet and the dryland farming in the north of ancient China as well as the dryland farming across Eurasia.

兴隆沟遗址全景（敖汉旗农牧局 / 提供）
Whole Scene of Xinglonggou Site (Provided by AAHB)

敖汉旗境内还发掘出“小河西文化”（距今 8 200 年以上）、“兴隆洼文化”（距今 7 400~8 200 年）、“赵宝沟文化”（距今 6 400~7 200 年）、“红山文化”（距今 5 000~6 700 年）、“小河沿文化”（距今 4 500~5 000 年）等文化遗址。它们的发现填补了中国东北地区考古编年的空白，并将中国北方地区新石器时代的历史向前推进了 3 000 年。此外，在这些遗址地都发现了与旱作农业相关的生产工具，如锄形器、铲形器、刀、磨盘、磨棒、斧形器等，其见证了敖汉旗的农业起源和农业发展历程。

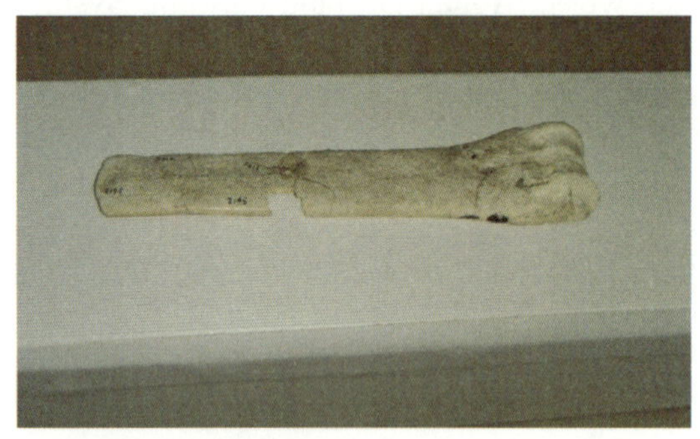

小河西遗址出土的骨制复合工具
（敖汉旗农牧局 / 提供）
Composite Tool Made of Bone Unearthed in Xiaohexi Site (Provided by AAHB)

兴隆洼遗址出土的石磨盘和磨棒
（敖汉旗农牧局 / 提供）
Millstone and Burnisher Unearthed in Xinglongwa Site (Provided by AAHB)

丰富的农作物品种

敖汉旗是典型的旱作农业区和农牧交错带，以粟和黍为代表的旱作农业系统不仅有着丰富的农业生物多样性，还保存了丰富多样的地方品种，对于农作物种质资源的保护具有重要意义。

敖汉旗的主要粮食作物是玉米、谷子、高粱、荞麦等。杂粮生产是当地的优势产业，有谷子、黍子、糜子、荞麦、高粱、杂豆等。谷子是仅次于玉米的第二大粮食作物，也是第一大杂粮作物。谷子在敖汉旗各地均有种植，主要有齐头白、五尺（1 尺≈ 33.3 厘米。全书同）高、二白谷、独秆紧、叉子红、花花太岁、绳子紧、兔子嘴、长脖雁、金镶玉、老来白、老虎尾等 50 余种地方品种。当地生产的谷子加工后的小米有 4 种颜色，分别是澄澄的黄、淡然的白、低调的绿和素雅的黑。不同颜色的小米有着不同的口感，营养成分也各有不同。敖汉旗的黍子也有很多地方品种，如大粒黄、大支黄、大白黍、小白黍、大红黍、疙瘩黍、高粱黍等。敖汉旗的高粱也有很多地方品种，如大青米、关东青、大白高粱、小青米、大红高粱、黏高粱等。此外，糜子、黑豆、绿豆、红豆、豇豆等均有不少地方品种仍在种植。

谷子地方品种——金镶玉（敖汉旗农牧局 / 提供）
Local Variety of Millet: *Jinxiangyu* (Provided by AAHB)

Ancient cultural relics have been discovered in Aohan Banner, such as "Xiaohexi Culture" (8200 years ago), "Xinglongwa Culture" (about 7400-8200 years ago), "Zhaobaogou Culture" (about 6400-7200 years ago), "Hongshan Culture" (about 5000-6700 years ago) and "Xiaoheyan Culture" (about 4500-5000 years ago). The discovery of the above cultural relics has not only filled an archaeological chronological gap in the northeast of China, but also pushed the history of the Neolithic period in the northern part of China 3000 years ahead. Besides, the instruments of production related to the dryland farming such as hoe-shaped tools, shovel-shaped tools, knives, millstones, burnishers and axe-shaped tools are also discovered in these relic areas. The discovery of these instruments of production has witnessed the agricultural origin and the agricultural development history in Aohan Banner.

Rich Crop Varieties

Aohan Banner is a typical dryland farming area and agro-pastoral transition zone. The dryland farming system which is represented by the millet and the broomcorn millet not only has rich agricultural biodiversity, but also preserves many different kinds of local varieties, which is of great significance for the protection of the crop germplasm resources.

The main food crop in Aohan Banner includes the corn, the millet, the sorghum and the buckwheat, etc. The coarse grain production is the advantage industry in Aohan Banner. The coarse grain includes the millet, the broomcorn millet, the proso millet, the buckwheat, the sorghum and the beans, etc. The millet is the second most important food crop after the corn and the most important coarse grain. The millet is planted all over Aohan Banner, having more than 50 local varieties such as *Qitoubai*, *Wuchigao*, *Erbaigu*, *Duganjin*, *Chazihong*, *Huahuataisui*, *Shengzijin*, *Tuzizui*, *Changboyan*, *Jinxiangyu*, *Laolaibai* and *Laohuwei*, etc. The local millet has four colors such as the orange yellow, slight white, low-key green, simple and elegant black. The millet in different color has different taste and nutritional ingredient. The broomcorn millet in Aohan Banner also has many local varieties such as *Dalihuang*, *Dazhihuang*, *Dabaishu*, *Xiaobaishu*, *Dahongshu*, *Gedashu* and *Gaoliangshu*, etc. The sorghum planted in Aohan Banner also has many local varieties such as *Daqingmi*, *Guandongqing*, *Dabaigaoliang*, *Xiaoqingmi*, *Dahongliang* and *Niangaoliang*, etc. Besides, some local varieties such as the proso millet, the black bean, the mung bean, the red bean and the cowpea are still planted in Aohan Banner.

黍子地方品种——大红黍（敖汉旗农牧局 / 提供）
Local Variety of Broomcorn Millet: *Dahongshu*
(Provided by AAHB)

传统的农业生产方式

敖汉旗的粟和黍是原始的栽培种，在区域分布和种植季节上具有互补性和不可替代性，而且生育期短、适应性强、耐旱、耐瘠薄，是当地重要的旱作作物选择。当地人采取垄作和梯田种植以粟和黍为代表的旱作作物，在粟和黍等旱作作物的种植上积累了丰富的经验。

由于粟和黍等旱作作物多生长在旱坡地上，且株型较小，不便于机械化作业，千百年来当地人保持着牛耕人锄的传统耕作方式。例如，在敖汉旗谷子播种仍先用马或驴拉犁开沟，再用当地称作点葫芦头的点种器点种。点种完后，把农家肥均匀地撒在播种沟内，然后及时覆土，防止跑墒，接着再用磙子镇压 2~3 遍，播种才结束。又如，间苗时仍通过人工把苗间开，并用小锄头把杂草除去，起到松土作用；中耕时人工锄草 3 遍以上，并通过锄头松土起到抗旱保墒的作用。

春播（敖汉旗农牧局 / 提供）
Spring Sowing (Provided by AAHB)

间苗（敖汉旗农牧局 / 提供）
Thinning Out Seedlings (Provided by AAHB)

Traditional Agricultural Production Methods

The millet and the broomcorn millet in Aohan Banner are the primitive cultivated species, which are complementary and irreplaceable with regard to the regional distribution and the planting seasons. They are the important dryland crops in Aohan Banner thanks to their short growing period, strong adaptability, drought-enduring and barren resistance characteristics. The local people adopt the ridge culture and build terraces to plant these dryland crops which are represented by the millet and the broomcorn millet. They have accumulated rich experience in planting the dryland crops such as the millet and the broomcorn millet.

Since the dryland crops such as the millet and the broomcorn millet are planted on the dry sloping field and their plant types are small, it is impossible to adopt the mechanized operation. Therefore, the local people have stuck to the traditional tillage method that cattle are used to plough the land while people hoe the land for thousands of years. For example, when Aohan people sow the millet, they usually use horses or donkeys to make furrows first, and then they dibble seeds with a kind of seed planter called Dianhulutou by local people. After dibbling seeds, they scatter the farmyard manure evenly on the furrows, and then they cover the soil on the furrows immediately to prevent the loss of moisture. Next, they grind the land for twice or three times with a roller and sowing is finished finally. For another example, when Aohan people thin out seedlings, they still thin the seedlings out manually; at the same time, they use a small hoe to get rid of weeds in order to loosen the soil; during the intertillage, people hoe up weeds for more than three times manually and loosen the soil with a hoe to fight a drought and prevent the loss of moisture.

当地人还保持着轮作倒茬、间作套种等传统生产方式，不仅提高了土壤肥力，还起到控制病虫害的作用。例如，谷子连作不仅容易导致病害严重、杂草多，还会导致土壤养分失调，因此当地人采用黍子—马铃薯—谷子—豆类的轮作方式，以调节土壤养分、恢复地力、减少病虫草害；玉米与其他作物间作，通过秸秆的遮阴作用，可抑制杂草的生长，减少病虫的寄生源头，从而减少了某些病虫害。另外，多种作物的间作套种还形成了独特的旱作农业景观。

由于多施用积造的农家肥，少施或不施化肥，多采用生物技术防治病虫害，无过量农药和化肥残留之忧，敖汉旗的杂粮品质是其他地区无法比拟的。敖汉旗也因此赢得了“中国杂粮出赤峰，绿色杂粮在敖汉”的美誉。

谷子与高粱间作（敖汉旗农牧局 / 提供）
Intercropping of Millet and Sorghum (Provided by AAHB)

旱作农业景观（敖汉旗农牧局 / 提供）
Dryland Farming Landscape (Provided by AAHB)

The local people still preserve the traditional planting methods such as the crop rotation and the intercropping, which can not only improve the soil fertility, but also control pests and diseases. For example, the continuous cropping of the millet can lead to the serious disease and more weeds as well as the maladjusted soil nutrients. Therefore, the local people adopt the crop rotation method of the broomcorn millet-potato-millet-beans in order to adjust the soil nutrients, recover the soil fertility and reduce pests and diseases as well as the weed encroachment. When the intercropping of the corn and other crops is adopted, the corn stalk can overshadow other crops, which can suppress the growth of weeds and reduce the parasitic source of diseases and pests, therefore reducing some diseases and pests. Besides, the intercropping of many kinds of crops has also formed a unique dryland farming landscape.

The quality of coarse grain of Aohan Banner is incomparable in that the crops there are mainly fertilized by farm manure accumulated by local people with less or no chemical fertilizers, and the biotechnology is applied to prevent pests and diseases without worrying about the excessive pesticide and fertilizer residue. Thanks to its high coarse grain quality, Aohan Banner has also won a reputation that "the best coarse grain in China is produced in Chifeng, and the green coarse grain is produced in Aohan.".

浓郁的旱作农耕文化

粟和黍等旱作作物的田间管理比较复杂，从春耕前的耙压保墒到开犁播种，到出苗后的耙压抗旱、人工间苗、除草追肥，再到成苗后的铲耘灌耥、灭虫，直到收割入场。在这一系列环节中，蕴含着的是传承数千年的农耕技艺和智慧。

长期的农业耕作实践经历数千年的积淀，也形成了丰富多彩、具有地方特色的旱作农耕文化。庙会、祭天、祭火、祭敖包、祭星、祈雨、撒灯等祈福习俗以及扭秧歌、踩高跷、唱大戏、呼图格沁（蒙古族傩剧）、跑黄河等民俗活动被世代传承下来。它们都和农耕文化有着密切的联系，大都是为了祈求一年的风调雨顺和五谷丰登以及庆祝丰收。

撒龙灯（敖汉旗农牧局 / 提供）
Salongdeng (Provided by AAHB)

祭星许愿（敖汉旗农牧局 / 提供）
Star Worship for Wishes (Provided by AAHB)

Rich Dryland Farming Culture

The field managementof the dryland crops such as millet and the broomcorn millet is very complicated, from grinding the soil and keeping the moisture of the soil, to the ploughing and sowing, to grinding to fight against drought, thinning seedlings out manually and weeding as well as topdressing after the seedling emergence, then to loosening the soil and the irrigation as well as the deinsectization after the grown-up seedlings, till the harvest. These series of steps reflect the farming skills and wisdom which have been inherited by local people for thousands of years.

Thanks to thousands of years' accumulation of long-term farming practices, rich and coloful dryland farming culture with local characteristics has gradually formed. The blessing customs such as the temple fair, the heaven worship, the fire worship, Aobao worship, the star worship, the rain-praying ceremony and Sadeng, and the folk activities such as Yangko, walking on stilts, singing folk operas, Hutugeqin (Nuo drama of Mongolian nationality) and Paohuanghe have been passed down from generation to generation in Aohan Banner. They are all closely related to the farming culture, most of which aim to pray for good weather for the crops, for a bumper grain harvest and to celebrate harvest.

CHAPTER 2 第2章

The Road to GIAHS

敖汉的申遗之路

春耕（敖汉旗农牧局 / 提供）
Spring Plouging (Provided by AAHB)

敖汉旱作农业系统的申遗之路源于一次特别的考古。2001—2003 年，敖汉旗境内的兴隆沟遗址进行了三次科学考古发掘，考古人员在这个保存较好的新石器时代聚落遗址发现了碳化粟和黍。经证实，这些碳化粟和黍是当今世界上所知较早的人工栽植形态的谷物。专家们由此推断，西辽河上游地区是粟和黍的起源地之一，是中国古代北方旱作农业的起源地之一，也是横跨欧亚大陆旱作农业的发源地之一。

考古结果出来以后，敖汉旗于 2010 年年底在北京召开了兴隆沟遗址考古发掘座谈会。会上，组织并指导了这批碳化谷物浮选工作的中国社会科学院考古研究所的赵志军研究员提及了联合国粮食及农业组织（FAO）正在开展的全球重要农业文化遗产（GIAHS）工作。敖汉旗领导敏锐地觉察到这是一次难得的机遇，提议积极申报。

2011 年 3 月，敖汉旗政府派出代表参加了由 GIAHS 中国项目办公室在北京举办的“农业文化遗产地农产品开发与管理研讨会”。会议期间，敖汉旗时任副旗长邢和平与项目办公室主任、中国科学院地理科学与资源研究所研究员闵庆文就敖汉旱作农业系统申报 GIAHS 问题进行了交流，并委托闵庆文研究员团队负责申遗材料的准备。这标志着敖汉旱作农业系统申报 GIAHS 工作正式启动。

敖汉旗把申遗工作作为旗委、旗政府工作的头等大事之一，专门成立了敖汉旱作农业系统申报 GIAHS 领导小组和办公室，多次召开会议对申遗工作进行安排部署。在专家团队的大力支持和帮助下，《敖汉旱作农业系统 GIAHS 申报书》于 2012 年年初完成，并通过农业部（现农业农村部）报送 FAO-GIAHS 秘书处。

丰收画卷（敖汉旗农牧局 / 提供）
Harvest Picture (Provided by AAHB)

The road to GIAHS of Aohan Dryland Farming System originated from a special archaeological excavation. From 2001 to 2003, the scientific archaeological excavation in Xinglonggou Site of Aohan Banner was carried out for three times and the millet carbide and the broomcorn millet carbide were unearthed in this well-protected Neolithic settlement site. It is proved that the millet carbide and the broomcorn millet carbide in Aohan Banner are known as the early cereal planted by people now in the world. Experts, based on the above discovery, infer that the upstream area of West Liaohe River is one of the origin areas of the millet and the broomcorn millet and the dryland farming in the north of ancient China as well as the dryland farming across Eurasia.

After the archaeological result was published, Aohan Banner held a forum on the archaeological excavation in Xinglonggou site in Beijing at the end of 2010. At this meeting, Prof. Zhao Zhijun at Institute of Archaeology of Chinese Academy of Social Sciences, who organized and guided the selection of these carbide grains, came up with the Globally Important Agricultural Heritage System (GIAHS) which was carried out by Food and Agriculture Organization of the United Nations (FAO). Aohan Banner government realized it a golden opportunity, and keenly and actively proposed to apply for it.

In March 2011, Aohan Banner participated in the “Seminar on Agricultural Products Development and Management in Agricultural Heritage Sites” in Beijing held by the project office of GIAHS in China. During the meeting, Mr. Xing Heping, then deputy head of Aohan Banner, discussed with Prof. Min Qingwen of Institute of Geographic Sciences and Natural Resources Research, Chinese Academy of Sciences, who was also the director of the project office, on the application for GIAHS of Aohan Dryland Farming System. The team of Prof. Min Qingwen was then entrusted to be responsible for the preparation for materials needed for the application for GIAHS. It marks the start-up of the application for GIAHS of Aohan Dryland Farming System officially.

The application for GIAHS was regarded as one of the top priorities of Aohan Banner party committe and government. As a result, leading group was set up specially for the application for GIAHS and meetings were held for several times to arrange the application for GIAHS. With the great support and help of the expert team, *Aohan Dryland Farming System GIAHS Proposal* was finished at the beginning of 2012. And it was submitted to the secretariat of FAO-GIAHS by the Ministry of Agriculture (current Ministry of Agriculture and Rural Affairs) of the People’s Republic of China.

在申遗材料准备和报送的同时，敖汉旗对外积极宣传，提高敖汉旱作农业系统的知名度；对内广泛动员，增强民众在遗产申报中的参与度。参加 2011 年 6 月在北京召开的“第三届全球重要农业文化遗产国际论坛”，邀请 FAO 驻中国、蒙古、朝鲜办事处代表 Percy Misika 先生于 2011 年 12 月到敖汉旗实地考察，参加 2012 年 3 月农业部（现农业农村部）主办的“中华农耕文化展”，与 FAO-GIAHS 中国项目办联合于 2012 年 8 月“首届中国兴隆洼文化节”期间举办“全球重要农业文化遗产地摄影作品展”。

为了让全旗人民都了解 GIAHS 申报工作、支持 GIAHS 申报工作，2011 年 4 月敖汉旗组织了以“人文敖汉，魅力敖汉，绿色敖汉”为主题的送文化下乡活动。活动突出展示了敖汉旗源远流长、光辉灿烂的历史文化，受到广大农牧民的热情欢迎。通过把 GIAHS 内容融入文艺节目中，GIAHS 申报工作的重要意义得到广泛宣传，全旗上下形成了积极参与、共同支持申遗工作的良好氛围。

2012 年 8 月 18 日，FAO-GIAHS 项目协调员 Parviz Koohafkan 先生致函中国项目办闵庆文研究员，同意将敖汉旱作农业系统列入 GIAHS 保护试点。2012 年 9 月 5 日，“全球重要农业文化遗产保护试点授牌仪式”在北京人民大会堂隆重举行。在时任农业部副部长牛盾先生等的见证下，时任 FAO 助理总干事 Alexander Muller 先生和 FAO-GIAHS 指导委员会主席李文华院士向敖汉旗旗委书记邱文博颁授 GIAHS 保护试点牌匾。敖汉旗成为当时内蒙古自治区唯一一个全球重要农业文化遗产地。2013 年 5 月，敖汉旱作农业系统被农业部（现农业农村部）列为首批中国重要农业文化遗产（China-NIAHS）。敖汉旗成为当时内蒙古自治区唯一获此殊荣的地区。

“全球重要农业文化遗产”英文牌匾（敖汉旗农牧局 / 提供）
GIAHS Plaque in English (Provided by AAHB)

When the application materials for GIAHS was prepared and submitted, Aohan Banner was actively publicizing the Aohan Dryland Farming System in order to improve its popularity and mobilizing people in Aohan Banner to participate in the application for GIAHS widely. In June 2011, Aohan Banner sent its representatives to participate in "The 3rd International Forum on Globally Important Agricultural Heritage Systems" held in Beijing. Aohan Banner invited Mr. Percy Misika, representative of FAO in the office of China, Mongolia and North Korea, to investigate Aohan Banner on-site in December 2011. Aohan Banner participated in the "Chinese Farming Culture Exhibition" sponsored by the Ministry of Agriculture (current Ministry of Agriculture and Rural Affairs) of the People's Republic of China in March 2012. Aohan Banner jointly held "GIAHS Photography Exhibition" during "The 1st Xinglongwa Cultural Festival of China" with the project office of FAO-GIAHS in China in August 2012.

In order to make people all over Aohan Banner learned about and support the application for GIAHS, Aohan Banner held activities to send culture to the countryside themed "Civilized Aohan, Appealing Aohan and Green Aohan" in April 2011. The long-standing and glorious history and culture in Aohan Banner were highlighted through these activities, which were also warmly welcomed by local farmers and herdsmen. The significance of application for GIAHS was widely publicized by integrating GIAHS contents into the cultural programs. As a result, Aohan Banner created a good atmosphere that people all over Aohan Banner actively participated in and jointly supported the application for GIAHS.

On August 18, 2012, Mr. Parviz Koohafkan, the coordinator of FAO-GIAHS project, wrote to Prof. Min Qingwen, director of the project office in China, saying that it was agreed that Aohan Dryland Farming System be listed into GIAHS pilots. On September 5, 2012, "Awarding Ceremony of Pilot Globally Important Agricultural Heritage Systems" was held ceremoniously in Beijing Great Hall. Mr. Niu Dun, then vice-minister of the Ministry of Agriculture, witnessed together with others that Mr. Alexander Muller, then assistant director-general of FAO and Academician Li Wenhua, the chairman of FAO-GIAHS steering committee, jointly granted GIAHS pilot plaque to Mr. Qiu Wenbo, the secretary of party committee of Aohan Banner. Aohan Banner became the only GIAHS site in Inner Mongolia Autonomous Region at that time. In May 2013, Aohan Dryland Farming System was listed into the first batch of China Nationally Important Agricultural Heritage Systems (China-NIAHS) by Ministry of Agriculture (current Ministry of Agriculture and Rural Affairs) of the People's Republic of China. Aohan Banner became the only area acquiring this great honor in Inner Mongolia Autonomous Region at that time.

《敖汉旱作农业系统保护与发展规划》封面（敖汉旗农牧局 / 提供）

Cover of *Conservation and Development Planning of Aohan Dryland Farming System* (Provided by AAHB)

整个申遗过程不足两年的时间，敖汉每一步都走得很坚定和扎实。然而，农业文化遗产的保护与发展不能止步于此。敖汉旗深知申遗成功只是开始，如何传承和保护敖汉旱作农业系统才是关键。为此，敖汉旗将农业文化遗产的保护工作纳入政府的议事日程，邀请专家编制《敖汉旱作农业系统保护与发展规划》，成立专门机构，安排专门经费。敖汉旗农业遗产保护与开发管理局（正股级）于 2013 年 3 月正式成立，2016 年 1 月更名为敖汉旗农业文化遗产保护中心（副科级），专门负责农业文化遗产保护与发展措施的落地实施。

在遗产的保护与传承上，敖汉旗特别重视传统作物品种、乡村文化等在遗产系统中的特殊价值。通过逐村推进的方式对传统品种进行收集与整理，并积极开展传统品种的推广应用和种质资源的科学研究；在全旗各乡镇组织“农耕记忆讲述”活动，在中小学开展优秀农耕文化宣传普及活动；加强非物质文化遗产的挖掘与保护，设立专门资金支持建设敖汉旗旱作农业展览馆。

敖汉旱作农业展览馆一角（武文杰 / 摄）

A Corner of Aohan Dryland Farming Exhibition Hall (Taken by Wu Wenjie)

Although the whole application for GIAHS lasted for no more than two years, Aohan Banner committed itself to the application firmly and steadily. However, the conservation and development of agricultural heritage can't stop here. Aohan Banner knows well that the success of the application for GIAHS is only a beginning. What matters is how to inherit and conserve Aohan Dryland Farming System. Therefore, Aohan Banner added the conservation of the agricultural heritage to its government agenda, invited experts to work out the *Conservation and Development Planning of Aohan Dryland Farming System*, set up a special institution and arranged special funds for the institution. The Administration Bureau of Agricultural Heritage Conservation and Development of Aohan Banner (stock level institution) was set up officially in March 2013, whose name was changed into Agricultural Heritage Conservation Center of Aohan Banner (vice-section institution) in January 2016. The institution is responsible for the implementation of measures on the agricultural heritage conservation and development wholly.

With regard to the conservation and inheritance of the heritage system, Aohan Banner attaches great importance to the special value of traditional crop varieties and rural culture in the heritage system. Aohan Banner collected and collated traditional varieties from each village, and actively carricd out the promotion and application of the traditional varieties and the scientific research on the germplasm resource. The "farming memory narration" activity was held in all towns of the banner. And the activity to publicize and popularize the excellent farming culture was held in the elementary and secondary schools in the whole banner. In order to enhance the exploration and protection of the intangible cultural heritage, special funds were arranged to build the dryland farming exhibition hall in Aohan Banner.

五彩庄稼地（敖汉旗农牧局 / 提供）
Multicolored Cropland (Provided by AAHB)

在遗产的发展与利用上，敖汉旗特别重视产业发展在遗产保护中的特殊作用。积极调整农业产业结构，将谷子种植面积由 2012 年的 40 万亩[①]提高到 2019 年的 92 万亩；加强绿色和有机生产基地的认证工作，制定谷子绿色、有机生产管理办法；采取“龙头企业 + 合作社 + 基地 + 农户”模式，实现生产、加工、储运、销售一体化；充分利用农业文化遗产的影响力，把敖汉小米培育成全国著名的区域公用品牌，演绎了“小米撬动世界，遗产大有可为”的佳话。经中国农业大学等单位评估，敖汉小米市场价值 113 亿元，市场影响力 72.39。

在遗产地能力建设上，敖汉旗通过多元途径开展宣传普及工作，“全球重要农业文化遗产”“全球环境 500 佳”“世界小米之乡”成为了当地农产品的三大金牌；连续举办六届世界小米大会，对敖汉小米起到重要宣传作用，提高了敖汉小米的国际知名度；实施创新人才孵化计划，鼓励农村青年返乡创业，涌现出一批支持农业文化遗产保护和小米产业发展的新农人。

---

① 1 公顷 =15 亩 1 ha = 15 are

With regard to the development and the utilization of the heritage system, Aohan Banner thinks highly of the special role that industrial development plays in the heritage conservation. Aohan Banner has actively adjusted its agricultural industrial structure and increased the planting area of the millet from 0.4 million mu in 2012 to 0.92 million mu in 2019. Aohan Banner has strengthened the certification of green and organic production bases and formulated the green and organic production and management methods of the millet. The banner has also adopted the model of "leading enterprises + cooperatives + production bases + farmers" to realize the integration of the production, processing, storage and transportation as well as the sales. By making a full use of the influence of the agricultural heritage, Aohan Banner has transformed Aohan millet into a famous regional public brand nationwide and created a much-told story that "millet can influence the world and the heritage can play an important role". After Aohan millet is evaluated by institutions including China Agricultural University, the market value of Aohan millet costs RMB 11.3 billion yuan and its market influence is 72.39.

With regard to the capacity building of the heritage site, Aohan Banner has publicized and popularized the heritage through different ways. The "Globally Important Agricultural Heritage Systems (GIAHS)", "Global 500 Roll of Honour for Environment Achievement" and the "Home of Millet in the World" have become three golden brands of local agricultural products. Six consecutive international conferences on the millet held in Aohan Banner have greatly publicized Aohan millet and improved its international reputation. Aohan Banner has implemented the innovation talent incubation program and encouraged rural youth to return to their hometown to start a business. In this way, many new farmers who support the agricultural heritage conservation and the millet industry development have sprung up in Aohan Banner.

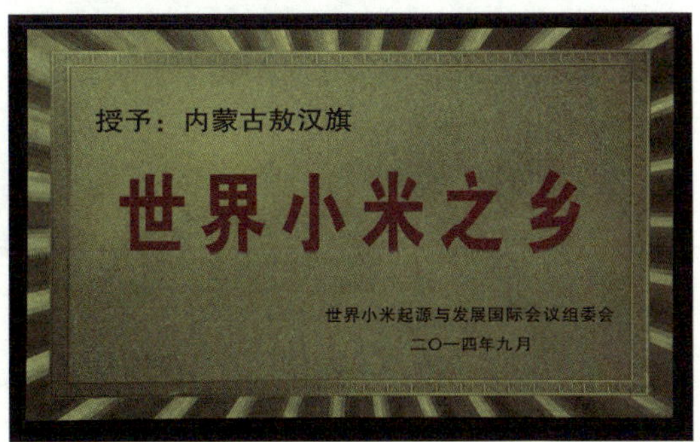

敖汉旗被授予"世界小米之乡"（敖汉旗农牧局／提供）
Aohan Banner Was Granted the Home of Millet in the World (Provided by AAHB)

经过多年的积极探索，敖汉旗成为中国北方地区农业文化遗产保护的先行者，敖汉小米品牌成为农业文化遗产保护与利用的成功案例。敖汉旗农业文化遗产保护中心徐峰和惠隆合作社理事长王国军于 2015 年分别荣获“全球重要农业文化遗产保护与发展贡献奖”和“全球重要农业文化遗产保护与发展突出贡献奖”。

徐峰获“全球重要农业文化遗产保护与发展贡献奖”（敖汉旗农牧局 / 提供）

Xu Feng Acquired “GIAHS Conservation and Development Contribution Award” (Provided by AAHB)

王国军获“全球重要农业文化遗产保护与发展突出贡献奖”（武文杰 / 摄）

Wang Guojun Acquired “GIAHS Conservation and Development Contribution Award” (Taken by Wu Wenjie)

After years of active exploration, Aohan Banner has become a forerunner of the agricultural heritage conservation in the northern area of China. Aohan millet brand has become a successful case of the agricultural heritage conservation and utilization. Mr. Xu Feng from Agricultural Heritage Conservation Center of Aohan Banner and Mr, Wang Guojun, the director-general of Huilong Cooperative were granted “GIAHS Conservation and Development Contribution Award” in 2015.

CHAPTER

3

第3章

Expert Opinions: Taste Aohan Millet

专家观点——品味敖汉小米

闵庆文　FAO GIAHS 科学咨询小组共同主席
Min Qingwen, Co-chair man of FAO GIAHS Scientific Advisory Group

对于小米，儿时的回忆有心酸也有甜蜜。那时因为生活贫困，小米只有在过年时才能吃到，留下的印象是黄澄澄、香喷喷。

今天吃小米，已经是作为健康饮食的重要组成部分。每晚一碗小米粥，于我几乎是一种习惯。

我国是小米的故乡，有许多著名的地域性品牌和商业性品牌，有各种有机、绿色、无公害认证。但我眼里的“敖汉小米”① 则与众不同，是因为她身上的另外两个标志：2002 年联合国环境规划署授予的“全球环境 500 佳”，2012 年联合国粮食及农业组织认定的“全球重要农业文化遗产”。前者说明了敖汉小米的生长环境，后者诠释了敖汉小米的历史演化。

从生态地理角度看，敖汉的确称得上“得天独厚”。位于农牧交错区的敖汉，四季分明，日照丰富，昼夜温差大，雨热同期，积温有效性高，是适宜优质黍粟生长的黄金地带。“南山、中丘、北沙”的地貌类型，加上富含硼、锌、铜、硒等微量元素的土壤，农产品质量不好都不可能，“中国杂粮出赤峰，绿色杂粮在敖汉”的美誉来自得天独厚的生态地理条件。也正是因为此，2014 年敖汉旗获得了中国作物协会粟类作物专业委员会授予的“全国最大优质谷子生产基地”称号。

---

① 闵庆文研究员撰写的“品味敖汉小米”原刊于《农民日报》2018 年 10 月 24 日第 8 版，后经整理收录 .
“Taste Aohan Millet” written by Prof. Min Qingwen was originally published on the 8th section of Farmers’ Daily on October 24, 2018. It is used here after being collated by authors.

When I was a child, I had the millet. At that time we were so poor that we could only eat the millet during the Spring Festival. In my memory, the millet was glistening yellow and sweet-smelling. When I think of the millet I ate as a child, I feel something sad but sweet.

Nowadays, we eat the millet, because it has become an important part of the healthy diet. I am now used to having a bowl of millet porridge every evening.

As the birthplace of the millet, China has many famous regional brands and commercial brands of the millet, as well as the organic, green and pollution-free certifications for the millet. However, in my mind, "Aohan millet" is quite different. It is because of its two signs: Aohan millet was granted the "Global 500 Roll of Honour for Environment Achievement" by United Nations Environment Programme in 2002; Aohan millet was rdesignated as the "Globally Important Agricultural Heritage Systems (GIAHS)" by Food and Agriculture Organization of the United Nations (FAO) in 2012. The former focuses on the growing environment of Aohan millet, while the latter explains the historical evolution of Aohan millet.

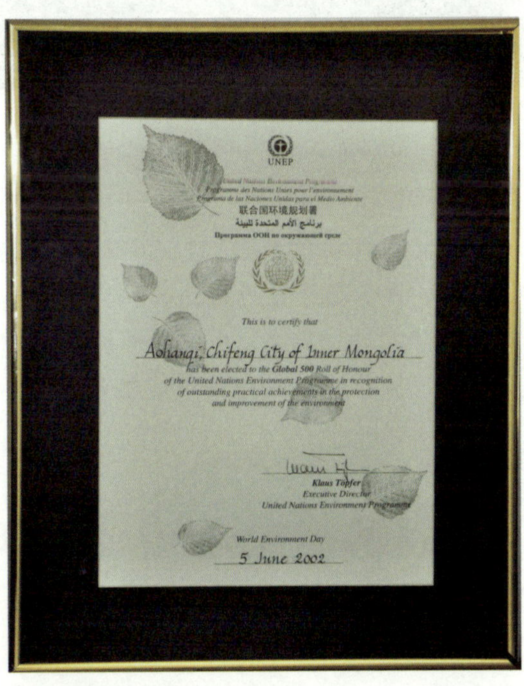

敖汉旗被授予"全球环境 500 佳"（敖汉旗农牧局 / 提供）
Aohan Banner Was Awarded the "Global 500 Roll of Honour for Environment Achievement" (Provided by AAHB)

锦绣山川（敖汉旗农牧局／提供）
Splendid Mountains and Rivers (Provided by AAHB)

从品种资源角度看，敖汉小米完全够得上“药食同源”。富含人体所需的氨基酸和钙、磷、铁等微量元素的敖汉小米，营养丰富，质纯味正，香软可口，既是平衡膳食、调节口味的理想食品，更是营养进补、身体恢复的最佳选择。耐干旱、抗倒伏、适应性强、品质优良的特点，可能是其 2013 年获得原国家质检总局地理标志产品的主要原因。

From the ecological and geographic perspectives, Aohan "enjoys exceptional advantages". Aohan, located at the agro-pastoral transition zone, has four distinctive seasons and plenty of sunshine. The temperature there varies widely from day to night. Besides, the rain and heat come during the same period there. Aohan also has high accumulative temperature efficiency. Thanks to all these favorable conditions, Aohan lies at a golden zone suitable for the growth of the high quality millet and broomcorn millet. Due to its advantageous geomorphic type of "mountains in the south, hills in the middle and sands in the north" and its soil rich in microelements such as boron, zinc, copper and selenium, the quality of agricultural products planted in Aohan is inevitably high. The reputation that "the best coarse grain in China is produced in Chifeng and the green coarse grain is produced in Aohan" comes from its unique ecological and geographic conditions. That's the reason why Aohan Banner acquired the title of "The Largest Production Base of High Quality Millet in China" granted by the Specialized Committee on Millet Crop of Crop Science Society of China in 2014.

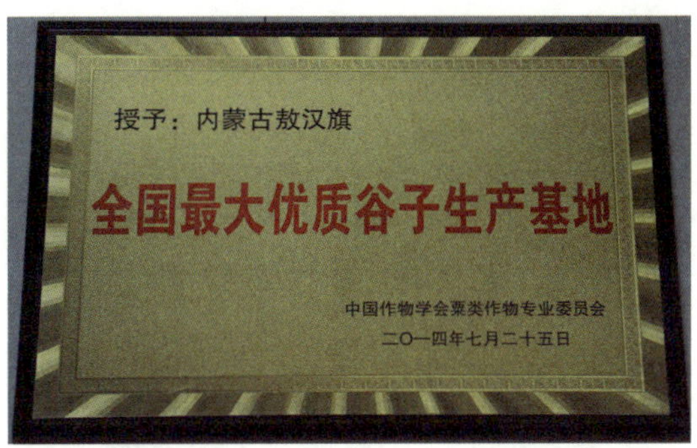

敖汉旗被授予全国最大优质谷子生产基地（敖汉旗农牧局／提供）
Aohan Banner Was Granted the Title of "The Largest Production Base of High Quality Millet in China" (Provided by AAHB)

From the perspective of variety resources, Aohan millet is good enough to meet the requirement of "homology of medicine and food". Aohan millet is not only rich in microelements such as amino acid, calcium, phosphorus and iron needed by people, but also full of nutrients, high quality, soft and delicious. It is the ideal food to keep a well-balanced diet and adjust the taste and the best choice to supplement nutrition and recover the health. Its characteristics such as the drought resistance, lodging resistance, strong adaptability and high quality may be the main reason why Aohan millet was regarded as the National Protected Geographical Indication Product by the former General Administration of Quality Supervision, Inspection and Quarantine in 2013.

敖汉小米被批准为国家地理标志保护产品（敖汉旗农牧局／提供）
Aohan Millet Was Approved as the National Protected Geographical Indication Product (Provided by AAHB)

镇压保墒（敖汉旗农牧局 / 提供）
Grinding to Keep the Moisture of the Soil (Provided by AAHB)

薅地（敖汉旗农牧局 / 提供）
Hoeing (Provided by AAHB)

收割（敖汉旗农牧局 / 提供）
Harvesting (Provided by AAHB)

冬藏（敖汉旗农牧局 / 提供）
Storing Millet in Winter (Provided by AAHB)

从历史文化角度看，敖汉小米堪称“活着的文物”。2003 年，考古工作者在敖汉旗兴隆沟发掘出了粟和黍的碳化标本，为敖汉小米 8 000 年历史提供了有力的证据。敖汉也因此获得了“中国古代旱作农业的起源地”的称号。

从农作方式角度看，敖汉小米可以说是“天然有机纯手工”。以小米为代表的敖汉杂粮大部分种植在山坡地和旱坡地上，农民们世世代代沿袭着施农家肥、间作套种、镇压保墒、人工除草等传统的耕作方式，有效减少了化肥和农药可能造成的农田污染。正可谓“敖汉杂粮，悉出天然”。

因为工作的原因，我去过敖汉多次，每次都有新的感受，也越发喜爱这个地方。我爱敖汉，是因为她有悠久的历史、灿烂的文化，因为她有美丽的田野、豪放的人民，还因为她有蕴含远古农耕文明基因、历经 8 000 年风雨而不衰的小米。

From the perspective of history and culture, Aohan millet can be called as the "living cultural relic". In 2003, the archaeological team unearthed the millet carbide and the broomcorn millet carbide at Xinglonggou in Aohan Banner, which has provided a powerful evidence for 8000-year-long history of Aohan millet. As a result, Aohan has gained the title of "origin area of dryland farming in ancient China".

From the perspective of the farming methods, Aohan millet is "natural, organic and pure handmade". Most Aohan coarse grains which are represented by the millet are planted on the hilly land and the dry slope land. Farmers in Aohan Banner have preserved the traditional farming methods such as applying the farmyard manure, the intercropping, grinding to keep the moisture of the soil and manual weeding that are inherited by them from generation to generation. These methods have effectively reduced the potential farmland pollution caused by the chemical fertilizer and the pesticide. It is what we say "Aohan coarse grains are all pure natural".

Thanks to my work, I have been to Aohan for several times. Each time I went there, I feel something new. The more I went there, the deeper I love this area. I love Aohan not only because she has a long history and magnificent culture, beautiful fields, bold and unconstrained people, but also because she has ancient farming civilization gene and the enduring millet with an 8000-year-long history.

闵庆文研究员（右二）在敖汉旗调研（敖汉旗农牧局 / 提供）
Prof. Min Qingwen (Second from Right) Is Investigating in Aohan Banner (Provided by AAHB)

四色小米（敖汉旗农牧局 / 提供）
Millet in Four Colors (Provided by AAHB)

实际上，我们也看到了一些改变，如航天育种、众筹种田、电商销售、休闲农业、小米音乐会，等等。但变的是形式，不变的是内涵，是 8 000 年以一贯之的生物与文化的遗传基因和精神、信仰与文化，是至今仍然传承着的传统的小米品种、传统的耕作技术、传统的加工工艺、传统的饮食文化和传统的乡土文化。

我曾经很肤浅地把饮食分为四个阶段：吃饱、吃好、吃健康、吃文化。而且认为，我们目前正处于第三阶段，即将步入第四阶段。正因为敖汉小米凝聚了 8 000 年世代劳动人民的心血与智慧，于我，已经不再是“吃食品”，而是“品文化”，因为她是“有文化内涵的生态农产品”的典型代表。

“敖汉”系蒙古语，其汉语意思是“老大”。祝愿“敖汉小米甲天下”成为现实，祝愿敖汉旱作农业系统这一世界上第一个也是目前唯一一个以传统旱作为主体的全球重要农业文化遗产保护好、传承好、利用好，成为世界农业文化遗产保护与发展的样板。

小米美食（敖汉旗农牧局 / 提供）
Delicious Food Made of Millet (Provided by AAHB)

In fact, we have also seen some changes, such as the space mutation breeding, the crowdfunding farming, e-commerce sales, leisure agriculture and millet concert, etc. However, what changes is the form instead of the content that is the genetic genes of biology and culture, the sprits, the belief and the culture for 8000 years, the traditional millet variety inherited till now, the traditional farming methods, the traditional processing techniques, the traditional food culture and the traditional countryside culture.

I once superficially classified the diet into four stages: getting enough to eat, eating well, eating healthily and tasting the food culture. Moreover, I think we are in the third stage now and we will move into the fourth stage soon. It is because Aohan millet has accumulated the laboring people's painstaking efforts and wisdom for 8000 years that having Aohan millet for me is not "having food" but "tasting the culture". It is the typical representative of the "ecological agricultural product with cultural connotation".

"Aohan" is Mongolian, which means "the first" in Chinese. I wish the idea that "Aohan millet is the best in the world" can be realized. I also wish Aohan Dryland Farming System, which is the first and the only GIAHS focusing on the traditional dryland farming in the world, can be protected, inherited and utilized well and will become a model in the agricultural heritage conservation and development in the world.

丰收时节（敖汉旗农牧局 / 提供）
Harvest Moment (Provided by AAHB)

Part Ⅱ 第二篇

Conservation and Inheritance of the Heritage System

遗产保护与传承

CHAPTER 1 第1章

Exploration and Inheritance of Archaeological Values

考古价值挖掘与传承

敖汉农耕文明演化

在敖汉 8 300 平方千米的土地上，分布着不同时期的古代遗址点 4 000 余处，居全国县级之首。其中，兴隆洼、兴隆沟、赵宝沟、草帽山、大甸子、城子山、燕长城、武安州、降圣州 9 处遗址被列为全国重点文物保护单位。境内发现有距今近万年前延续至 3 000 年前的 7 种考古学文化，分别是小河西文化、兴隆洼文化、赵宝沟文化、红山文化、小河沿文化、夏家店文化和夏家店上层文化。其中，小河西文化、兴隆洼文化、赵宝沟文化和小河沿文化是以敖汉地名命名。

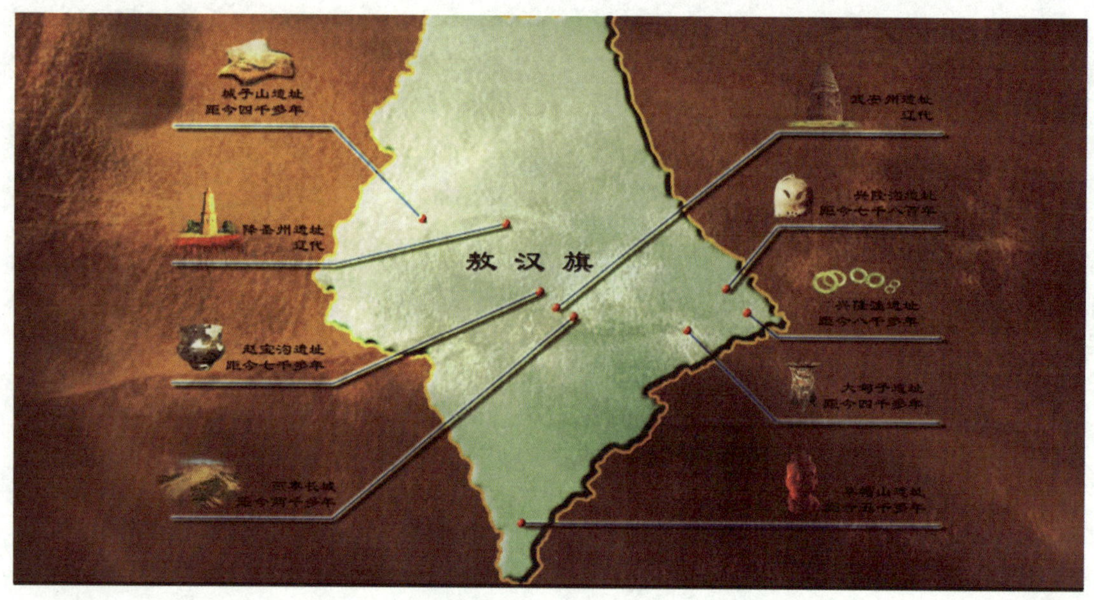

史前遗址分布（敖汉旗农牧局 / 提供）
Distribution of Prehistoric Sites (Provided by AAHB)

兴隆洼遗址的发现，添补了我国东北地区新石器时代考古编年的空白，将中国北方新石器时代的编年史向前推进了 3 000 年。这里的考古学文化谱系齐全、脉络清晰、没有缺环，被学术界誉为是“中国北方乃至东北亚地区史前文化研究的中心”，是文明太阳升起的地方。“龙祖玉源”“华夏第一村”“中华祖神”，一个个耀眼的光环，让敖汉旗蜚声中外。

Evolution of Aohan's Agricultural Civilization

There are more than 4000 ancient sites in different ages scattered on the land of Aohan Banner with 8300 square kilometers, the most of all counties in China. Among them, 9 sites such as Xinglongwa, Xinglonggou, Zhaobaogou, Caomaoshan, Dadianzi, Chengzishan, Yan Great Wall, Wu'anzhou and Xiangshengzhou are listed as the national key cultural relic protection units. Seven kinds of archaeological culture such as Xiaohexi culture, Xinglongwa culture, Zhaobaogou culture, Hongshan culture, Xiaoheyan culture, Xiajiadian culture and Upper Xiajiadian culture inherited from nearly 10000 years to 3000 years ago are discovered in Aohan Banner. Among them, Xiaohexi culture, Xinglongwa culture, Zhaobaogou culture and Xiaoheyan culture are named after places in Aohan Banner.

The discovery of Xinglongwa Site has not only filled an archaeological chronological gap in the northeast part of China during the Neolithic period, but also pushed the chronicles of the Neolithic period in the northern part of China 3000 years ahead. Due to the complete pedigree, clear sequence of thought without any missing link, it is honored as "the center of the research on the prehistoric culture in the northern China and Northeast Asian region" by the academics and the place where the civilization develops. Many titles such as "a place where the earliest dragon fossil in China and the earliest jade ware in the world are discovered", "the first village in ancient China" and "Chinese ancestral God" have made Aohan Banner known at home and abroad.

兴隆洼遗址发掘（敖汉旗农牧局 / 提供）
Excavation of Xinglongwa Site (Provided by AAHB)

兴隆沟红山文化聚落遗址（敖汉旗农牧局提供）
Hongshan Culture Settlement Site in Xinglonggou (Provided by AAHB)

在兴隆洼文化时期，狩猎采集经济占据主导地位，但在兴隆沟遗址首次发现经过人工栽培的碳化粟，表明当时已经出现了原始的农业经济；至红山文化和夏家店下层文化时期，农业经济开始成为主导性经济，狩猎采集经济作为补充。从距今 8 000 年前的兴隆洼文化、赵宝沟文化，发展到距今 5 000~6 000 年前的红山文化，再到后来的小河沿文化、夏家店下层文化，展示了远古时代敖汉旗地区农业经济及其文化起源与发展的基本线索。

大量古老的与旱作农业相关的生产生活工具，见证了敖汉旗的旱作农业萌芽于“小河西”，发展于“兴隆洼”，辉煌于“红山”，传承于“夏家店”，延续到“元明清”。与长江中下游地区以种植水稻为特点的稻作农业起源相比，北方旱作农业包括黍和粟的人工培植受到的关注鲜少。事实上，旱作农业体现了中华民族对人类文明发展作出的突出贡献。

During Xinglongwa cultural period, hunting and gathering economy played an important role. However, the discovery of the millet carbide planted manually in Xinglonggou Site for the first time proves that the primitive agricultural economy came into being at that time. During Hongshan culture and Lower Xiajiadian culture periods, the agricultural economy became the leading economy, while hunting and gathering economy became supplementary. The development from Xinglongwa culture and Zhaobaogou culture 8 000 years ago, to Hongshan culture 5 000 or 6 000 years ago, to the subsequent Xiaoheyan culture and Lower Xiajiadian culture, shows a basic clue of the agricultural economy and its cultural origin and development in ancient times in the area of Aohan Banner.

Lots of production and living tools related to the ancient dryland farming witnessed the beginning of the dryland farming of Aohan Banner from “Xiaohexi”, the development of it at “Xinglongwa”, the boom of it at “Hongshan”, the inheritance from “Xiajiadian” and the continuation to “Yuan, Ming and Qing Dynasties”. Compared with the rice farming origin in the middle and lower reaches of Yangtze River where the rice is planted mainly, the dryland farming in the north including the artificial planting of the millet and the broomcorn millet has been seldom noticed. In fact, the dryland farming has indicated the prominent contribution made by the Chinese nation to the development of the human civilization.

红山文化遗址地出土的石耜、石棒头（敖汉旗农牧局 / 提供）
Shisi and Shibangtou Unearthed at Hongshan Culture Site (Provided by AAHB)

赵宝沟遗址地出土的石耜（敖汉旗农牧局 / 提供）
Shisi Unearthed at Zhaobaogou Site (Provided by AAHB)

揭秘粟黍之源

以种植粟和黍为代表的北方旱作农业是中国农业起源的两个发展脉络之一。北方旱作农业的代表作物粟和黍，是长期适应北方干旱环境逐步演变而来的。长期以来，由于缺乏充足的植物遗存实物资料，关于粟类作物的起源问题一直没有得到权威的佐证。直到 21 世纪初，敖汉旗境内的兴隆沟遗址的考古发掘才为确定北方旱作农业起源提供了重要线索。

2001—2003 年，中国社会科学院考古研究所、敖汉旗博物馆和日本青森县合作，在敖汉旗兴隆沟遗址进行了大规模发掘。中国社会科学院考古研究所赵志军研究员，以植物考古学专家身份参与了敖汉旗兴隆沟遗址的考古挖掘和价值认定工作。他带领考古队采用植物考古田野方法——浮选法，先后采集了浮选土样约 1 500 份，从中发现了 1 500 多粒碳化粟和黍。其中，黍占 90%，粟占 10%。

敖汉旗兴隆沟遗址（敖汉旗农牧局 / 提供）
Xinglonggou Site in Aohan Banner (Provided by AAHB)

Expose the Source of Millet and Broomcorn Millet

The dryland farming in the north China which is represented by the planting of the millet and the broomcorn millet is one of two development processes of the Chinese agriculture origin. The millet and the broomcorn millet, as the representative crops of the dryland farming in the north, have gradually evolved by adapting to the arid environment in the north for a long time. Due to the lack of sufficient physical information on the plant remains for a long time, the source of the millet crops lacked the authoritative evidence. Until the beginning of the 21st century, the archaeological excavation at Xinglonggou Site within Aohan Banner has provided an important clue to the source of the dryland farming in the north of China.

From 2001 to 2003, the Institute of Archaeology of Chinese Academy of Social Sciences, Aohan Museum and Aomori-ken in Japan cooperated to carry out a large-scale excavation at Xinglonggou Site in Aohan Banner. Prof. Zhao Zhijun of the Institute of Archaeology of Chinese Academy of Social Sciences participated in the archaeological excavation and the value identification work at Xinglonggou Site in Aohan Banner as a plant archaeologist. He led the archaeological team to adopt the field method of the plant archaeology - the flotation method. They collected about 1500 samples of the flotation soil successively, from which they found more than 1500 grains of the millet carbide and the broomcorn millet carbide, with 90% of the broomcorn millet and 10% of the millet.

兴隆沟遗址出土碳化黍粒（敖汉旗农牧局 / 提供）
Broomcorn Millet Carbide Unearthed at Xinglonggou Site (Provided by AAHB)

兴隆沟遗址地出土的炭化粟（敖汉旗农牧局 / 提供）
Millet Carbide Unearthed at Xinglonggou Site (Provided by AAHB)

经中国社会科学院考古研究所植物考古实验室和美国哈佛大学、加拿大多伦多大学以 C14 手段检测论证，认为这些碳化的粟和黍是人工栽培的标本，是中国北方最早的农作物种子，距今 7 700—8 000 年，比欧洲地区发现的粟早 2 700 年，这奠定了敖汉旗作为旱作农业起源地之一的重要历史地位。由此，兴隆沟遗址被学术界定为横跨整个欧亚大陆旱作农业的发源地之一。

敖汉旗被授予“中国小米之乡”（敖汉旗农牧局 / 提供）
Aohan Banner Was Granted as the “Home of the Millet in China” (Provided by AAHB)

2014 年 9 月，中国社会科学院考古研究所、英国剑桥大学麦克唐纳考古研究所、中国作物协会粟类作物专业委员会、敖汉旗人民政府共同举办了“第一届世界小米起源与发展国际会议”。世界各国考古、农业文化遗产和谷子体系研究领域的顶级专家经过充分论证形成共识：敖汉旗是世界小米之乡，是谷子起源地之一。2014 年 10 月，中国粮食行业协会授予敖汉旗“中国小米之乡”。

After the Plant Archaeology Laboratory of the Institute of Archaeology of Chinese Academy of Social Sciences, Harvard University in America and University of Toronto in Canada jointly tested the millet carbide and the broomcorn millet carbide with C14, they believed that the millet carbide and the bromcorn millet carbide were the specimens planted manually and the earliest crop seeds in the north of China 7700 to 8000 years ago, 2700 years earlier than those discovered in European area. It has proved the important historical position of Aohan Banner as one of the dryland farming origins. From then on, Xinglonggou Site has been regarded as one of the dryland farming origins across the whole Eurasia by the academic circle.

In September 2014, the Institute of Archaeology of Chinese Academy of Social Sciences, the MacDonald Institute for Archaeological Research of the Cambridge University in UK, the Specialized Committee on Millet Crop of Crop Science Society of China and Aohan Banner People’s Government jointly held “The 1st International Conference on the Source and Development of the Millet in the World”. The top experts in the fields of archaeology, agricultural heritage and millet from countries worldwide, based on full demonstration, reached the consensus that Aohan Banner was the home of the millet in the world and one of the origin areas of millet. In October 2014, China National Association of Grain Sector granted Aohan Banner the “Home of the Millet in China”.

CHAPTER 2 第2章

Collection and Collation of Traditional Varieties

传统品种收集与整理

政府引导传统品种收集

丰富的农业物种资源和生物多样性是农业文化遗产系统的重要特征之一。品种多样性的保护对于农业文化遗产的保护与传承具有至关重要的作用。自 2013 年以来，敖汉旗政府通过逐村推进的方式对传统品种进行收集与整理。调查人员每到一户都组织填写《传统品种种植情况调查表》，并对每个品种单独装袋，分别建卡，卡内包括该品种的农家俗名、生长性状、抗病性、抗逆性等信息。调查人员还对每个品种保留地做了空间定位，以此绘制了传统品种分布图，从而摸清了传统品种的分布信息。

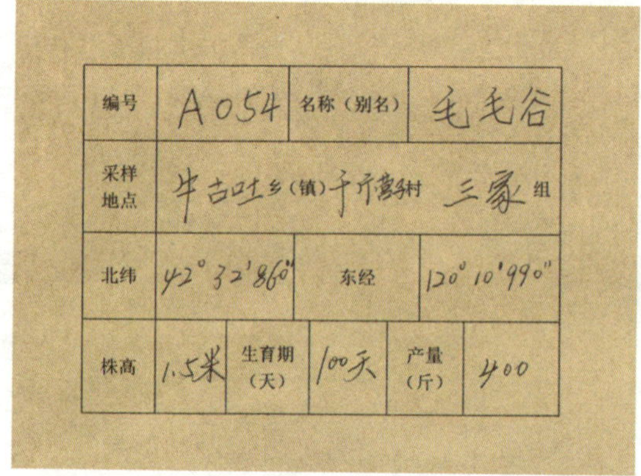

编号	A054	名称（别名）	毛毛谷		
采样地点	牛古吐乡（镇）千斤营村 三家 组				
北纬	42°32'860"	东经	120°10'990"		
株高	1.5米	生育期（天）	100天	产量（斤）	400

传统品种登记卡（敖汉旗农牧局 / 提供）
Registration Card of the Traditional Varieties (Provided by AAHB)

谷子地方品种——毛毛谷（敖汉旗农牧局 / 提供）
Local Variety of Millet: Maomaogu (Provided by AAHB)

入户收集传统品种（敖汉旗农牧局 / 提供）
Collecting Traditional Varieties at Farmers' Houses (Provided by AAHB)

2013 年敖汉旗政府先后完成了兴隆洼、古鲁板蒿、玛尼罕、丰收、四家子、牛古吐等具有杂粮种植传统乡镇的地方传统品种收集整理工作，入户近 500 家，共收集到谷子、玉米、高粱、黍子、芝麻、糜子等的地方传统品种 103 个。2014 年在玛尼罕、下洼、金厂沟梁等乡镇收集传统品种 26 个。2015 年在木头营子、羊场办事处等地收集传统品种 54 个。2016 年在贝子府镇、长胜镇等地收集传统品种 35 个。2013—2016 年，敖汉旗在全旗范围内共收集到谷子、玉米、黍子、高粱、荞麦等传统品种 218 个，其中谷子传统品种 92 个。敖汉旗政府与农业科研院所联合攻关，对旗内传统品种资源进行实物和电子数据整理，建立了全国第一个旗县级旱作农业种质资源库。

Government Guided the Collection of the Traditional Varieties

Rich germplasm resources and biological diversity is one of the important characteristics of the agricultural heritage systems. The protection of the variety diversity plays an important role in the conservation and inheritance of the agricultural heritage systems. Aohan Banner government has collected and collated the traditional varieties from village to village since 2013. When the investigators visit a farmer's house, they need to complete the *Questionnaire Form on the Planting of the Traditional Varieties* and put each variety in a different pocket, and then they need to make a card for each variety to record the information such as the local name, the growth characteristics, the disease resistance and the stress resistance. The investigators have also reserved a space positioning of each variety, based on which they can draw a distribution diagram of the traditional varieties. In this way, they have figured out the distribution information of the traditional varieties.

In 2013, Aohan Banner finished the collection and collation of the traditional varieties at towns and townships which have a tradition to plant the coarse grain such as Xinglongwa Town, Gulubanhao Township, Manihan Township, Fengshou Town, Sijiazi Town and Niugutu Town. The investigators visited nearly 500 farmers' houses and collected 103 traditional varieties, including the millet, the corn, the sorghum, the broomcorn millet, the sesame and the proso millet, etc. In 2014, they collected 26 traditional varieties at Manihan Township, Xiawa Town and Jinchanggouliang Town, etc. In 2015, they collected 54 traditional varieties at Mutouyingzi Township and Yangchang Administrative Area, etc. In 2016, they collected 35 traditional varieties at Beizifu Town and Changsheng Town, etc. From 2013 to 2016, Aohan Banner totally collected 218 traditional varieties such as the millet, the corn, the broomcorn millet, the sorghum and the buckwheat all over the banner, of which there are 92 traditional varieties of the millet. Aohan Banner government and the agriculture research institutions jointly collated the physical resources and the electronic data of the traditional varieties collected within the banner and established the first seed bank of the dryland farming at the banner and county level in China.

工作人员收集传统品种（敖汉旗农牧局 / 提供）
Investigators Were Collecting Traditional Varieties (Provided by AAHB)

多方参与传统品种收集

除了政府的持续推动以外，传统品种的收集与整理也离不开农民、科研人员等的参与合作。中国科学院农业政策研究中心牵头开展了近 20 年的“参与式选育种试验”，让科研人员能够与农民共同参与、密切合作，从而满足农民需求、强化农民种子系统、解决育种遗传资源基础狭窄、农作物生物多样性减少等问题。中国科学院农业政策研究中心研究员宋一青和国际生物多样性中心研究员罗尼曾多次赴敖汉旗调研传统品种，深入兴隆洼镇大甸子村、嘎岔村与农民进行座谈，详细了解了当地种植的农作物种类、品种、品种来源以及传统品种的留种方式，并计划在敖汉旗建立种子银行，加强对当地种质资源和生物多样性的保护。

宋一青研究员（右一）在敖汉旗调研（敖汉旗农牧局 / 提供）
Prof. Song Yiqing (First from Right) Was Investigating in Aohan Banner (Provided by AAHB)

小粒荞麦（敖汉旗农牧局 / 提供）
Small Buckwheat (Provided by AAHB)

Multi-stakeholder Participation in the Collection of the Traditional Varieties

In addition to the continuous advancement of the government, farmers and researchers also participated in the collection and collation of the traditional varieties. The Center for Chinese Agricultural Policy of Chinese Academy of Sciences led to carry out nearly 20-year-long "Participatory Seed Selection and Breeding Experiment", which enabled the researchers to jointly participate in the work with farmers. The close cooperation between the researchers and farmers can satisfy farmers' needs, strengthen farmer seed system and solve problems such as limited foundation of the breeding genetic resources and the decline in the crop biodiversity. Song Yiqing, a researcher of Center for Chinese Agricultural Policy of Chinese Academy of Sciences, and Ronnie, a researcher of Biodiversity International, visited Aohan Banner to investigate the traditional varieties many times. They talked with farmers at Dadianzi Village and Gacha Village of Xinglongwa Town to learn about the type and the variety of local crops, and the source of the variety as well as the method to preserve the traditional varieties in detail. Besides, they planned to set up a seed bank in Aohan Banner to enhance the conservation of the local germplasm and the biodiversity.

鹏程农业繁育基地（敖汉旗农牧局 / 提供）
The Breeding Base of Pengcheng Agriculture (Provided by AAHB)

马鹏程、卢瑞香夫妇出生于敖汉旗良种繁殖场，从小就对农作物育种感到新奇。多年以后，这对夫妇办起自己的种子公司——敖汉旗鹏程农业发展有限公司（简称“鹏程农业”）。这是一家集科研、繁育、开发为一体的民营高科技企业，最初以经营两杂作物种质为主。在敖汉旱作农业系统获得全球重要农业文化遗产认定之后，在敖汉旗农业文化遗产保护中心的支持下，公司开展了传统品种搜集、保护、开发与利用工作。截至2019年年底，公司已搜集到传统品种89个，涉及谷子、玉米、高粱、黍子、豆类等10多种农作物，并利用这些传统品种开展了新品种选育和推广工作。例如，公司通过南繁北育，开发了抗性好、产量高的高粱新品种新杂2号，并在东北、内蒙古、宁夏回族自治区（全书简称宁夏）等地推广。凭着对良种繁育的热爱，鹏程农业充分利用自身优势，积极参与传统品种的保护与传承，让这些散落民间的老种子重新焕发了生机。

The couple named Ma Pengcheng and Lu Ruixiang were born in a breeding farm for improved varieties in Aohan Banner. They have been interested in the crop breeding since they were children. After many years, the couple founded their own seed company - Aohan Banner Pengcheng Agricultural Development Co., Ltd (hereinafter referred to as Pengcheng Agriculture). It is a privately owned high-tech company, which integrates scientific research, breeding and development. At the beginning of its foundation, the company mainly engaged in the seeds of hybrid rice and hybrid corn. After Aohan Dryland Farming System was designated as GIAHS, the company carried out the collection, conservation, development and utilization of traditional varieties with the support of Agricultural Heritage Conservation Center of Aohan Banner. As of the end of 2019, the company has collected 89 traditional varieties, including more than 10 kinds of crops such as the millet, the corn, the sorghum, the broomcorn millet and beans, etc. The company has also carried out the breeding and promotion of new varieties by means of these traditional varieties. For example, the company has developed the new variety of the sorghum - Xinza No.2. It has good resistance and high yield through the method of reproducing in the south and breeding in the north. And the new variety has been promoted in the northeastern area of China, Inner Mongolia Autonomous Region and Ningxia Autonomous Region. Based on the enthusiasm in the breeding for improved varieties, Pengcheng Agriculture has made full use of its own advantages and participated in the conservation and inheritance of the traditional varieties in an effort to rejuvenate the old seeds scattered in local area.

高粱（敖汉旗农牧局 / 提供）
Sorghum (Provided by AAHB)

敖汉旱作农业系统品种保护基地（敖汉旗农牧局 / 提供）
The Variety Protection Base of Aohan Dryland Farming System (Provided by AAHB)

品种保护基地鸟瞰（敖汉旗农牧局 / 提供）
The Airview of the Variety Protection Base (Provided by AAHB)

传统品种分区栽培（敖汉旗农牧局 / 提供）
Traditional Varieties Are Planted in Different Plots (Provided by AAHB)

工作人员测量谷子穗长（敖汉旗农牧局 / 提供）
Staff Were Measuring the Length of the Millet Ear (Provided by AAHB)

建设传统品种保护基地

在传统品种收集整理的基础上，敖汉旗自2014年开始建设敖汉旱作农业系统品种保护基地，这可能也是第一个位于全球重要农业文化遗产地的品种保护基地。基地集传统品种保护和新品种引进于一体，采用农业气象自动观测系统，对温度、湿度、风速、风向、雨量、全辐射6个气象要素进行实时监测，对作物所处生育期、作物覆盖度、密度等参数进行全天候、智能化的自动化观测，通过高分辨率图像传感器，实现作物长势自动识别和图像分析处理，为试验数据获取提供了科技保障。该基地设置农作物虫情测报灯，对于害虫发生量和发生期的测报准确率大大提高，为旱作作物虫害防治提供科学依据。

2014年，敖汉旗完成建设传统品种试验基地25亩，试验种植谷子品种313个，为建立全国首家旗县级旱作农业种质资源库打下了坚实的基础。2015年，完成建设传统品种试验繁育基地16亩，种植品种170个，其中，传统品种151个，扩繁谷子品种12个，实施谷子育种6个，对照谷子品种1个。2016年，完成建设基地17亩，包括藜麦品种引进试验区、传统杂粮杂豆品种保护区、鹰嘴豆品种引进试验区、传统大豆品种保护区、传统谷子品种保护区、传统谷子品种繁育区、传统玉米品种保护区、传统高粱品种保护区和谷子新品种引进试验区共8个区。种植15种作物371个品种，其中，引进藜麦品种4个，鹰嘴豆品种152个，谷子品种160个；种植传统谷子品种21个，荞麦、黍谷、糜子、绿豆等品种共计22个，玉米品种2个，高粱品种4个，油葵品种1个；繁育传统谷子品种2个，大豆品种3个。与此同时，敖汉旗安排专门技术人员，实施无缝隙田间跟踪管理，并做好每个品种从播种到成熟的全程数据记录。

Build a Protection Base of Traditional Varieties

Based on the collection and collation of the traditional varieties, Aohan Banner has begun to build the variety protection base of Aohan Dryland Farming System since 2014, which is probably the first traditional variety protection base in GIAHS sites. The base has integrated the protection of the traditional varieties and the introduction of the new varieties. The agrometeorological automatic observation system has been used to supervise the six elements of meteorology such as the temperature, the humidity, the wind velocity, the wind direction, the rainfall and the total radiation in real time. The system can carry out an all-weather and intelligent observation of the parameters such as the current growing period of the crop, the crop coverage and the density automatically. The image sensor with high resolution can automatically identify the crop growth, analyze and process the image, which provides a scientific guarantee for the access to the experiment data. The base has also set up a crop insect detection lamp, which can greatly improve the forecasting accuracy of the occurrence amount and the emergence period concerning the pest in an effort to provide scientific basis for the pest control of the dryland crops.

In 2014, Aohan Banner finished the construction of the traditional variety experimental base taking up an area of 25 mu, where 313 kinds of millet were planted for experiment. It laid a solid foundation for establishing the first germplasm resources gene bank for the dryland farming at the banner and county level in the country. In 2015, Aohan Banner built the experimental breeding base of the traditional variety, taking up an area of 16 mu, where 170 varieties were planted. Among them, there were 151 traditional varieties, 12 propagation millet varieties, 6 breeding millet varieties and 1 control millet variety. In 2016, Aohan Banner built the base taking up an area of 17 mu which included 8 plots such as the introduction and test plot of the quinoa variety, the protection plot of traditional coarse grain and mixed beans varieties, the introduction and test plot of the chickpea variety, the protection plot of traditional soybean variety, the protection plot of traditional millet variety, the breeding plot of traditional millet variety, the protection plot of traditional corn variety, the protection plot of traditional sorghum variety and the introduction and test plot of the new millet variety. In these plots, 371 varieties of 15 crops were planted. Among them, 4 quinoa varieties, 152 chickpea varieties and 160 millet varieties were introduced; 21 traditional millet varieties, 22 varieties of buckwheat, broomcorn millet, proso millet and mung beans, 2 corn varieties, 4 sorghum varieties and 1 oil sunflower variety were planted; 2 traditional millet varieties and 3 soybean varieties were bred. At the same time, Aohan Banner arranged dedicated technicians to conduct seamless field tracking management and record all data of each variety from sowing seeds to the maturity.

传统谷子品种保护区（敖汉旗农牧局 / 提供）
Protection Plot of Traditional Millet Varieties (Provided by AAHB)

截至 2019 年年底，敖汉旗共抢救濒危传统品种 32 个，为进一步筛选出品质好、产量高、抗病抗逆性强、适应当地气候土壤条件种植的旱作作物品种提供了良好基础。

此外，敖汉旗还将兴隆洼镇大窝铺村和新惠镇扎赛营子村确定为农业文化遗产监测点，对传统品种的保护利用等农业文化遗产保护与传承工作进行监测，并每年向农业农村部报送监测报告。

人们世代繁衍，种子代代相传，生产因此得以延续。附着在传统品种上的不仅仅是粮食产出的物质价值，还有丰富的遗传多样性和传承不息的农耕文化。传统品种的搜集、整理、保护与传承，功在当今，利在千秋。

As of the end of 2019, Aohan Banner has saved 32 endangered traditional varieties totally, which has provided a good foundation for the further selection of dryland crop varieties with high quality, high yield, strong disease resistance and stress resistance and suitable for local climate and soil conditions.

Besides, Aohan Banner has regarded Dawopu Village of Xinglongwa Town and Zhasaiyingzi Village of Xinhui Town as monitoring sites to monitor the conservation and inheritance of the agricultural heritage system, such as the conservation and utilization of traditional varieties. Aohan Banner submits the monitoring report to the Ministry of Agriculture and Rural Affairs of the People's Republic of China every year.

Just as people multiply their off-springs, seeds are passed down from generation to generation, which makes it possible to keep the production. The traditional varieties can not only create physical value of grain yield, but also pass down the rich genetic diversities and the inherited farming culture. The collection, collation, conservation and inheritance of the traditional varieties are not only significant currently, but also meaningful in the future.

CHAPTER 3

第 3 章

Conservation and Inheritance of Traditional Knowledge

传统知识保护与传承

探寻农耕文明，留下最美乡音

敖汉旗拥有 8 000 年农耕文明，传统农耕文化是敖汉先人们留下的得天独厚、不可复制的宝贵财富。敖汉旗的传统农耕文化，限于之前的挖掘投入不足，基本停留在老百姓的脑海里，在现有的文字资料中很难查到。因此，挽救性地开展传统农耕文化记录、挖掘 8 000 年文化精髓、为子孙后代留下宝贵历史资料十分必要和迫切。

2014 年 7 月，中国农业大学孙庆忠教授率领团队组建了全球重要农业文化遗产调研组，并驻扎敖汉旱作农业系统核心保护区——兴隆洼镇大窝铺村和大甸子村，开展“农耕记忆”讲述活动。调研组辗转走访敖汉旗 16 个乡镇 20 多个村庄，面对面采访农耕能手，深入田间地头实地考察玉米、高粱、谷子、黍子等旱作作物种植情况。调研组累计走访 50 多户农户，掌握了大量传统农耕器具和留种、开沟、点种、田间管理、收获、贮藏、加工等传统农耕技术的第一手资料，为复原 8 000 年的农耕文化奠定了坚实的资料基础。

孙庆忠教授（左一）开展农耕器具收集（敖汉旗农牧局 / 提供）
Prof. Sun Qingzhong (First from Left) Was Collecting Farming Tools (Provided by AAHB)

调研组采访农耕能手（敖汉旗农牧局 / 提供）
The Research Group Was Interviewing Elite Farmers (Provided by AAHB)

Search for Farming Civilization and Keep the Best Voice

Aohan Banner boasts its 8000-year-long farming civilization. The traditional farming culture is a unique and irreproducible valuable asset passed down from ancestors of people living in Aohan Banner. The traditional farming culture of Aohan Banner was only reserved in people's mind due to previously insufficient input to collect it. It was difficult to find out something about it from existing literal data. Therefore, it is necessary and urgent to save and record the traditional farming culture and dig into the essence of the 8000-year-long culture in order to keep the valuable historical materials for further generations.

In July 2014, Prof. Sun Qingzhong from China Agricultural University set up a research group for GIAHS. The research group was stationed at the core protection area of Aohan Dry-land Farming System - Dawopu Village and Dadianzi Village of Xinglongwa Town, to carry out the narration activity of the "farming memory". The research group visited more than 20 villages of 16 towns and townships in Aohan Banner to interview the elite farmers face to face and investigate the planting of the dryland farming crops such as the corn, the sorghum, the millet and the broomcorn millet in the fields. The research group has accumulatively visited more than 50 farmers' houses and acquired the first hand information on lots of traditional farming tools and the traditional farming techniques such as reserving seed for planting, furrowing, dibbling, field management, harvest, storage and processing, etc. The work has laid a solid information foundation for the recovery of the 8000-year-long farming culture.

孙庆忠教授（左二）采访农耕记忆人（敖汉旗农牧局/提供）
Prof. Sun Qingzhong (Second from Left) Was Interviewing the Farmers (Provided by AAHB)

除了组织“农耕记忆”讲述活动，孙庆忠教授还组织开展了“农耕记忆”口述史编辑工作，旨在以人文社会科学角度介入，深入研究农业文化遗产保护与开发的现实意义，有效保护和传承传统农耕文化。在全旗范围内寻找到世代从事农业生产、熟知当地农耕技术、风俗习惯及各类农事活动的农耕记忆人 15 位，均是 70 岁以上。通过采访、录音、整理、存档入库等工作，有效地保护和传承了传统的农耕文化。

为不断丰富“农耕记忆”口述资料，2016 年，孙庆忠教授再次组建“农耕记忆”讲述采访组。对全旗 48 位 65 周岁以上的农耕能手进行采访，把留在他们脑海里的农耕记忆挖掘出来，将濒临灭绝的农耕文化以文字、音像的形式记录下来，采访组累计整理文字资料 20 多万字。

为了全面了解民众对敖汉旗传统农耕文化的认知程度，2014 年，孙庆忠教授团队针对 500 名义务教育阶段的 4~9 年级学生开展了“农业与农村认知问卷调查”活动。除了全面了解学生们对农村、农业生产、传统民俗等与农业文化遗产相关知识的认知程度，活动本身也是对传统农耕文化的直接宣传，有效提升了当地社会公众对优秀传统农耕文化的认知水平。

In addition to the organization of the narration activity of the "farming memory", Prof. Sun Qingzhong has also organized the editing work of the oral history of the "farming memory" to research the practical significance of the conservation and the development of the agricultural heritage system deeply and effectively conserve as well as inherit the traditional farming culture from the perspective of the humanities and social sciences. Prof. Sun Qingzhong found 15 farmers with good memory who engaged in the farming for generations, were familiar with local farming techniques, customs and activities related to the farming. All of the farmers interviewed were above 70 years old. Prof. Sun Qingzhong has effectively protected and inherited the farming culture by means of interviewing, recording, collating and filing for the storage, etc.

In order to continue to enrich the oral information of the "farming memory", Prof. Sun Qingzhong set up an interviewing group again in 2016. The group interviewed 48 elite farmers above 65 years old in the whole banner in order to dig up the farming memories remained in their mind and record the endangered farming culture in the form of text and audio as well as video. The group has totally collated more than 200000 words of the literal data.

In order to learn about local people's cognition degree toward the traditional farming culture of Aohan Banner comprehensively, Prof. Sun Qingzhong's team issued the "questionnaires on the cognition of the agriculture and countryside" to 500 students from Grade 4 to Grade 9 at their compulsory education stage in 2014. The team, through the questionnaire, has not only learned about students' cognition degree of the knowledge related to the agricultural heritage such as the countryside, farming and traditional customs, but also directly publicized the traditional farming culture, which has effectively improved the cognitive level of local people toward the outstanding traditional farming culture.

开展"农业与农村认知问卷调查"活动（敖汉旗农牧局 / 提供）

The Activity of "Questionnaire on the Cognition of the Agriculture and the Countryside" (Provided by AAHB)

传承农耕技艺，推动绿色种植

传统农耕知识与技术是传统农耕文化的重要组成部分，其保护与传承不仅仅需要专家学者以及当地政府的努力，更需要当地农民的亲身参与。采用传承千年的传统农耕技艺从事农业生产，是保护优秀传统农耕文化的重要途经。

在漫长的敖汉旱作农耕路上，先民们通过施用农家肥、轮作、套种等传统技术，从播前准备、播种到田间管理、收获，形成了一个完整的体系，实现了对土地的永续利用。然而，在现代社会，由于受经济利益的驱使，通过过量施用化肥农药以追求高产的现象比比皆是，选种、积肥、播种、土法防病虫等传统农耕技艺濒临失传。当然，并不是所有人都只顾眼前利益，越来越多的“勇敢的逆行者”加入到绿色种植队伍中来，敖汉旗谷哥杂粮种植农民专业合作社的发起人——李洪刚，就是其中的代表。

李洪刚在田间劳作（敖汉旗农牧局 / 提供）
Li Honggang Was Working in the Field (Provided by AAHB)

培土（敖汉旗农牧局 / 提供）
Hilling (Provided by AAHB)

2014 年，李洪刚发起成立了谷哥杂粮种植农民专业合作社，坚持以传统农业耕作技术种植传统作物品种。作物耕种时，用驴拉着犁，用传统农具“点葫芦头”播种；作物生长期内，坚持不使用化肥和农药，采用人力除草；作物收割后，用驴拉着碌子进行打场。截至 2019 年年底，合作社种植面积已经达到 320 亩，种植品种主要是敖汉旗传统的绿谷、黑谷等。

Inherit Farming Technique and Promote Green Planting

The traditional farming knowledge and techniques are the important components of the traditional farming culture. Their conservation and inheritance need not only the efforts of experts, scholars and local government, but also the actual participation of local farmers. Applying the traditional farming techniques inherited for thousands of years to the agriculture production is an important way to conserve the outstanding traditional farming culture.

On the long way to Aohan dryland farming, ancestors acquired and formed a complete farming system, from the pre-sowing preparation and sowing seeds to the field management, and realized the sustainable use of the land by means of the traditional techniques such as the application of the farmyard manure, the crop rotation and the intercropping. However, in modern society, people driven by the economic interests apply excessive chemical fertilizers and pesticides in pursuit of the high yield. As a result, the traditional farming techniques such as the seed selection, the manure collection, sowing seeds and the native method to prevent the crop disease and insects are endangered. Naturally, there are still some "brave contrarians". Li Honggang - the founder of Guge Coarse Grain Planting Farmers' Specialized Cooperative in Aohan Banner, is a representative of such contrarians.

In 2014, Li Honggang initiated and founded Guge Coarse Grain Planting Farmers' Specialized Cooperative. He insisted that the traditional farming techniques be used to plant the traditional crop varieties. When cultivating crops, he made donkey pull the plough and sowed seeds with the traditional farming tool called "Dianhulutou"; during the growing period of the crops, he insisted that chemical fertilizers and pesticides not be used. And he insisted on weeding fields manually; after the crops were reaped, he threshed grains with a donkey pulling a stone roller. Up to December 2019, the planting area of the cooperative has reached 320 mu and the planting varieties mainly include the traditional green millet and black millet of Aohan Banner.

人工除草（李洪刚 / 摄）
Weeding Manually (Taken by Li Honggang)

打场（敖汉旗农牧局 / 提供）
Threshing Grains (Provided by AAHB)

制作传统驱虫药水（李洪刚 / 摄）
Make Traditional Insect Repellent Water (Taken by Li Honggang)

谷哥杂粮种植农民专业合作社在运行中也遇到了不少困难和挑战。比如，由于不使用化肥和农药，主要靠人力去除草驱虫，劳动力投入大，生产成本增加多，作物也比较容易遭受病虫害的侵袭。为了应对病虫害，合作社也采用了一些传统的防治手段。比如，采用辣椒、大蒜和烟叶泡水后喷洒等生态环保措施。为了应对不同类型的病虫害，合作社也在不断探索，努力征集应对作物病虫害的方案，找到有效的传统方法，最大程度地降低病虫害的影响。

敖汉旱作农业系统的成功申遗，提高了谷哥杂粮种植农民专业合作社及其农产品的知名度，拓展了农产品的销售渠道。李洪刚和他的合作社表示，他们能做的就是保持初心，最大程度地采用传统农耕技术，让消费者吃到放心的粮食，以实际行动去保护和传承农业文化遗产。

Guge Coarse Grain Planting Farmers' Specialized Cooperative has also encountered many difficulties and challenges during its operation. For example, because the cooperative mainly wccds manually instead of the chemical fertilizers and pesticides, more labour forces are needed, which increases the production cost. And it is easier for the crops to suffer from diseases and pests. In order to prevent diseases and pests, the cooperative has also applied some traditional insect repellent methods. For example, they soak chili, garlic and the tobacco leaf in the water for a day first. Then, they splash such water on the leaves of crops to prevent the pests. In order to prevent different kinds of diseases and pests, the cooperative is also making efforts to collect methods in the hope of finding effective traditional methods to reduce, to the full extent, the impacts of diseases and pests.

The successful application for GIAHS of Aohan Dryland Farming System has greatly improved the popularity of Guge Coarse Grain Planting Farmers' Specialized Cooperative and its agricultural products, and expanded the marketing channels of its agricultural products. Li Honggang and his cooperative say that what they can do is to stay true to their original goal and apply the traditional farming techniques as much as possible. In this way, they hope consumers can eat healthy food. They are insisting on the conservation and inheritance of the agricultural heritage with their practical action.

CHAPTER 4 第4章

Conservation and Inheritance of Traditional Culture

传统文化保护与传承

延续敖汉血脉，传承非遗文化

敖汉旗先人们在长期的农业耕作中所创造的民间文化经过数千年的积淀与传承，逐步形成了具有地方特色的旱作农耕文化。传承至今的庙会、祭星、祈雨、撒灯、扭秧歌、踩高跷、唱大戏、呼图格沁（蒙古族傩剧）、黄河灯会等民俗活动就是敖汉旗旱作农耕文化的典型代表。

这些多样多彩的非物质文化，极大地丰富了人们的精神生活，成为社会稳定、文化发展的原动力。但随着人们生产、生活方式改变，大量从事农业生产的劳动力进城务工，这些活动的举办气氛、参与热情和参与人数都出现了明显的下滑。活动中蕴含的传统文化也渐渐被疏远，其继承和发扬后继乏人，有些甚至面临单传的窘境。建立非物质文化遗产保护机制，显得愈发迫切和重要。

青城寺蒙古族祭星（敖汉旗非物质文化遗产保护中心 / 提供）
Star Worship Activity of Mongolian Nationality at Qingcheng Temple (Provided by Intangible Cultural Heritage Conservation Center of Aohan Banner (hereinafter referred to as ICHCC))

呼图格沁（敖汉旗非物质文化遗产保护中心 / 提供）
Hutugeqin (Provided by ICHCC)

Continue the Flood Lines and Inherit the Intangible Cultural Heritages

After thousands of years' accumulation and inheritance, the folk culture created by ancestors of Aohan Banner during their long-term farming has gradually formed the dryland farming culture with local specialties. The folk activities such as the temple fair, the star worship, the rain-praying ceremony, Sadeng, Yangko, walking on stilts, singing folk operas, Hutugeqin (Nuo drama of Mongolian nationality) and Yellow River Lantern Festival which have been inherited so far are the typical representatives of the dryland farming culture in Aohan Banner.

The various kinds of intangible culture has greatly enriched people's spiritual life and become the motive power for the social stability and cultural development. However, with the change of people's production mode and lifestyle, lots of labour forces engaging in the agricultural production previously enter cities for job opportunities. As a result, the great decline can be seen in the activity atmosphere, participating enthusiasm and number of participants in these activities. The traditional culture contained in these activities is also gradually neglected. There is no successor to inherit and carry forward these activities. Some activities even face the dilemma of a single successor. Establishing the protection mechanism of the intangible culture heritage has become more and more important and urgent.

撒龙灯（敖汉旗非物质文化遗产保护中心 / 提供）
Salongdeng (Provided by ICHCC)

敖汉旗非物质文化遗产保护中心（以下简称非遗中心）是致力于非物质文化遗产保护的专门机构。截至 2019 年年底，非遗中心已成功申请自治区级非物质文化遗产 3 项，分别是呼图格沁、敖汉民间传说和青城寺蒙古族祭星，市级非物质文化遗产 12 项，旗级非物质文化遗产 52 项，对非物质文化遗产保护发挥了重要作用。在众多非物质文化遗产中，与敖汉旱作农业系统密切相关的呼图格沁、青城寺祭星、黄河灯会、敖汉拨面、小米主食制作技艺等均被较好地保护起来。

小米美食（敖汉旗农牧局 / 提供）
Millet Food (Provided by AAHB)

敖汉拨面（敖汉旗非物质文化遗产保护中心 / 提供）
Aohan Bomian (Provided by ICHCC)

完整传承是对非物质文化遗产最好的保护。非遗中心从这个角度入手，开启了遗产传承人的发掘登记工作。自 2008 年以来，非遗中心先后启动了对呼图格沁、青城寺祭星、黄河灯会、敖汉拨面、小米主食制作等非物质文化遗产传承人的发掘走访。截至 2019 年年底，已详细登记遗产传承人近 70 人，为保障这些遗产的传承奠定了坚实基础。

为加强对非物质文化遗产的保护，敖汉旗政府还设立了专门资金，支持建设敖汉旱作农业展览馆，全方位展示农耕器具、远古农业、民俗活动、传统品种等旱作农耕文化。展览馆于 2017 年 3 月 15 日对外开放，通过对旱作农耕文化的全面展示，彰显了全球重要农业文化遗产的魅力，成为人们了解和传承农业文化遗产的最好平台。

Intangible Cultural Heritage Conservation Center of Aohan Banner (hereinafter referred to as ICHCC) is a professional institution committing to the conservation of the intangible cultural heritages. As of December 2019, ICHCC has successfully applied for 3 intangible cultural heritages at the autonomous region level, such as Hutugeqin, Aohan folk legend and the star worship activity of Mongolian nationality at Qingcheng Temple, and 12 intangible cultural heritages at municipal level as well as 52 intangible cultural heritages at banner level. ICHCC has played an important role in the conservation of the intangible cultural heritage. Among many intangible cultural heritages, those related to Aohan Dryland Farming System such as Hutugeqin, the star worship at Qingcheng Temple, Yellow River Lantern Festival, Aohan Bomian, manufacturing skills of the millet staple food are also conserved well.

The complete inheritance is the best conservation for the intangible cultural heritage. Based on this, ICHCC started to look for the heritage successors. It has been looking for the successors of the intangible cultural heritage such as Hutugeqin, the star worship at Qingcheng Temple, Yellow River Lantern Festival, Aohan Bomian, manufacturing skills of the millet staple food successively since 2008. As of December 2019, about 70 heritage successors are registered by ICHCC, which has laid a solid foundation for guaranteeing the inheritance of these heritages.

In order to enhance the conservation of the intangible cultural heritages, Aohan Banner has set up a special fund to build Aohan dryland farming exhibition hall, where the dryland farming culture such as farming tools, ancient agriculture forms, folk activities and traditional varieties are displayed comprehensively. The exhibition hall was open to the public on March 15, 2017. The exhibition hall highlighted the charm of GIAHS by means of the comprehensive display of the dryland farming culture. It has become the best platform for people to learn about and inherit the agricultural heritage systems.

继承祖志，丰富生活

敖汉旗传承至今的非物质文化遗产类型不少，但当前最受欢迎、参与人数最多、体验最为丰富的还属黄河灯会。

黄河灯会，俗称“跑黄河”或“转九曲”，在清朝康熙年间从山西传入敖汉地区。这一民俗文化活动传承了两百多年，是敖汉旱作农业系统的重要组成部分。通过黄河灯会，人们将愿望上传给天地神灵，祈求五谷丰登、平安幸福。这一民俗文化活动丰富了人们的精神生活，对维护邻里和谐、维护社会稳定起了重要作用。2018 年 9 月，黄河灯会被赤峰市人民政府评为第四批非物质文化遗产。

黄河灯会得以传承，离不开一代又一代传承人的持续努力。孟祥志是黄河灯会的第四代传承人。从七八岁开始，他就跟在父辈后面学习灯会的布置，参与一些力所能及的活动，拿一拿秫秸靶子、挂一挂彩灯等。每次活动结束，他都有满满的收获。在他的记忆中，黄河灯会从来没有中断过，每年的灯会都热闹非常。如今，每年进入正月，孟祥志便组织村民出资出力，在平坦的地方用秫秸、麻绳、木桩等布设成 9、12 或 24 连城的“黄河阵”。每隔一定距离埋设 1 根木桩，桩与桩的顶部用 1 根秫秸连结，下部用两根交叉的秫秸相连，形成跑道隔墙。“跑黄河”者须沿跑道一气跑出，不许退出或穿“墙”而出，在进出口各放置牌楼 1 座，楼顶部各插 5 面彩旗，下悬 9 盏宫灯，门桩贴大红楹联，门侧挂三霄女和姜子牙画像。阵内各木桩上端亦同样悬灯挂旗。

黄河灯会现场（敖汉旗非物质文化遗产保护中心 / 提供）
Scene of Yellow River Lantern Festival (Provided by ICHCC)

Inherit Ancestors' Ambition and Enrich Nowdays Life

Although there are many intangible cultural heritages inherited so far, Yellow River Lantern Festival is the most popular one with the largest number of participants and the richest experience of all.

Yellow River Lantern Festival, also known as "Paohuanghe" or "Zhuanjiuqu", was introduced to Aohan area from Shanxi province during the Kangxi period in Qing Dynasty. This kind of folk activity, inherited for more than 200 years, is an important component of Aohan Dryland Farming System. Through Yellow River Lantern Festival, people express their wishes to the gods of heaven and earth praying for a bumper grain harvest, safety and happiness. This folk activity has not only enriched people's spiritual life, but also played an important role in maintaining the harmonious relationship among neighbors and the social stability. In September 2018, Yellow River Lantern Festival was regarded as the fourth batch of intangible cultural heritage by Chifeng Municipal Government.

Yellow River Lantern Festival should have not been inherited without continuous efforts made by one generation after another. Meng Xiangzhi is the fourth-generation successor of Yellow River Lantern Festival. He has learned the arrangement of Yellow River Lantern Festival from his father since he was seven or eight years old. He also participated in some activities within his limits, such as carrying the sorghum rods and hanging coloured lantern or lamp etc. He learns something new after each activity. In his memory, Yellow River Lantern Festival has never been suspended. The lantern festival is very boisterous each year. Nowadays, from the first month of the lunar year, Meng Xiangzheng organizes villagers to participate in the activity by contributing money or efforts. They work out the "Yellow River Array" linked to 9, 12 and 24 connections with sorghum rods, hemp rope and the timber pile on flat area. One timber pile is buried every certain distance. One sorghum rod is used to link the top of each timber pile, while the foot of the timber pile is linked with two crossed sorghum rods. Then the partition wall of the runways is formed. The participant of "Paohuanghe" has to run out of the array in one breath along runways and should neither exit nor cross the "walls". Otherwise, it will be deemed as the inauspicious behavior. One memorial archway is set up at entrance and exit respectively. 5 coloured flags are hung on the top of each memorial archway and 9 palace lanterns are hung in front of the memorial archway. Bright red couplets are put up on each side of the door. Pictures of Sanxiaonv and Jiang Ziya are hung on the doorjamb. Lamps and flags are also hung on the top of each timber pile in the array.

黄河灯会现场（敖汉旗非物质文化遗产保护中心 / 提供）
Scene of Yellow River Lantern Festival (Provided by ICHCC)

夜幕降临时，点燃灯火，灯会开始，即刻鼓乐、鞭炮齐鸣。秧歌队伍首先进入阵内，接着旱狮、旱船、跑驴、小车会鱼贯而入，最后是“跑黄河”的民众。人们在黄河阵中沿着曲曲弯弯的跑道奔跑、起舞，形成一股人的河流、欢乐的海洋。在“跑黄河”时，人们可乘机“拿”走小旗，回家后插在门窗上，意为“太公姜子牙令旗在此，邪祟不能近前”。“跑黄河”还有一个规矩，即必须连续举行三年，头一年叫“跑龙头”，第二年叫“跑龙身”，第三年称“跑龙尾”。如有中断，传说会引来旱魅，产生旱灾。在作物收成强烈依赖自然降水的农业社会，干旱是人们生存的最大敌人。为保证粮食的丰收，人们一直信奉并遵守着这个传统仪式。

When darkness falls, lights are turned on and the lantern festival began. Suddenly, drums are played and firecrackers are set off. The yangko team enters into the array first. Then, the lion model, the land boat model, the donkey model and the small car model follow the team. At last, people participating in “Paohuanghe” activity enter into the array. People run and dance happily along the twisting runways of the “Yellow River Array”. It’s a stream of people and the ocean of joy. When people participate in the “Paohuanghe” activity, they are allowed to “steal” a small flag. After they go home, they can hang the flag on the window of the door. It indicates that “Here is Taigong Jiang Ziya’s flag of command, and evil thing can’t get close to this house”. There is a rule in the “Paohuanghe” activity. The activity must be held three consecutive years. In the first year, the activity is called “dragon head”; the second year, it is called the “dragon body”; and the third year, it is called the “dragon tail”. If the activity is suspended, it will be deemed as inauspicious behavior. It is said that the suspension can attract Hanmei, a drought monster in ancient Chinese myth which can cause drought. In an agricultural society heavily depending on the natural rainfall, the drought is the greatest enemy for people’s survival at that time. In order to ensure a harvest of crops, people firmly believed in this rule.

Development and Utilization of the Heritage System

遗产发展与利用

CHAPTER 1 第1章

Study and Utilization of Germplasm Resources

种质资源研究与利用

推广应用传统品种

传统谷子品种——大红谷（敖汉旗农牧局 / 提供）
Traditional Millet Variety: Dahonggu (Provided by AAHB)

传统谷子品种——黄金苗（敖汉旗农牧局 / 提供）
Traditional Millet Variety: Huangjinmiao (Provided by AAHB)

种质资源的保护与利用是敖汉旱作农业系统可持续发展的根基。以粟和黍的种植为代表的敖汉旱作农业系统，时至今日还保存着丰富的传统品种资源。目前，敖汉旗种植的传统谷子品种有黄金苗、大金苗、大红谷、吨谷、小粟粮、老虎尾等 30 余种。其中，金苗和红谷两个传统品种得到重点推广，成为敖汉小米的核心品种，形成粥型品种黄金苗系列和饭型品种红谷系列。

在赤峰市农牧科学研究院的支持下，敖汉旗对传统农家品种进行选育、提纯和复壮。从传统谷子品种黄金苗选育出的新品种"敖谷 1 号"，在 2008—2009 年内蒙古自治区谷子品种区域试验中表现出较好的适应性，并于 2010 年 5 月通过内蒙古自治区谷子品种认定①。"敖谷 1 号"的推广应用获得"2017 年度内蒙古自治区农牧业丰收奖二等奖"。

① 徐峰，索良喜，王艳超，王显瑞，刘忠民．优质高产谷子品种敖谷 1 号的选育及高产栽培技术．种子，2018，37(6)：110 - 111．

Xu Feng, Suo Liangxi, Wang Yanchao, Wang Xianrui, Liu Zhongmin. Seed Selection and High-yield Cultivation Techniques of Quality Millet Variety Aogu No. 1 with High Yield. Seed, 2018, 37(6): 110-111.

Expand the Application of Traditional Varieties

The conservation and utilization of the germplasm resources are the foundation of the sustainable development of Aohan Dryland Farming System. Aohan Dryland Farming System which is represented by the planting of the millet and the broomcorn millet still reserves rich traditional variety resources till now. Currently, the traditional millet varieties planted in Aohan Banner include more than 30 varieties such as Huangjinmiao, Dajinmiao, Dahonggu, Dungu, Xiaosuliang, Laohuwei, etc. Among them, two traditional varieties such as Jinmiao and Honggu are selected as the core varieties of Aohan millet to be promoted mainly. Huangjinmiao series can be used as the porridge, while Honggu series can be used as the meal.

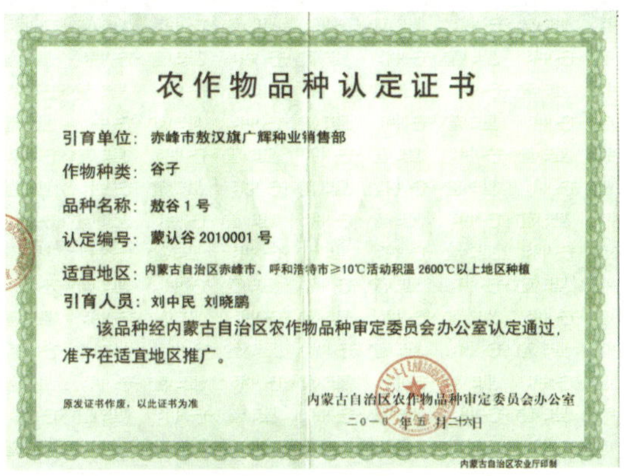
农作物品种认定证书

引育单位：赤峰市敖汉旗广辉种业销售部

作物种类：谷子

品种名称：敖谷 1 号

认定编号：蒙认谷 2010001 号

适宜地区：内蒙古自治区赤峰市、呼和浩特市≥10℃活动积温 2600℃以上地区种植

引育人员：刘中民 刘晓鹏

该品种经内蒙古自治区农作物品种审定委员会办公室认定通过，准予在适宜地区推广。

原发证书作废，以此证书为准

内蒙古自治区农作物品种审定委员会办公室

“敖谷 1 号”通过内蒙古自治区谷子品种认定（敖汉旗农牧局 / 提供）

“Aogu No. 1” Passed the Millet Variety Certification in Inner Mongolia Autonomous Region (Provided by AAHB)

With the support of Chifeng Agriculture and Animal Husbandry Science Institute, Aohan Banner has carried out the seed selection, purification and cultivation concerning the traditional variety. The new variety named “Aogu No. 1” bred from Huangjinmiao, the traditional millet variety, represented good adaptability in the regional experiment of millet varieties in Inner Mongolia Autonomous Region from 2008 to 2009. In May 2010, the new variety passed the millet variety certification4 in Inner Mongolia Autonomous Region. The promotion and application of “Aogu No. 1” was awarded “The 2nd Prize for Agricultural and Animal Husbandry Harvest in Inner Mongolia Autonomous Region in 2017”.

奖状

敖汉旗农业技术服务中心

“谷子新品种“敖谷1号”推广应用”项目获 2017 年度内蒙古自治区农牧业丰收奖 贰 等奖。你单位为第 01 完成单位。

特发此证。

编号：2017-2-01-121

“敖谷 1 号”获内蒙古农牧业丰收奖二等奖（敖汉旗农牧局 / 提供）

“Aogu No. 1” Was Awarded “The 2nd Prize for Agricultural and Animal husbandry Harvest in Inner Mongolia Autonomous Region” (Provided by AAHB)

赤谷 K1 试验地（敖汉旗农牧局 / 提供）
Experimental Field of Chigu K1 (Provided by AAHB)

赤峰市农牧科学研究院还以金苗为材料成功选育出金苗 K 系列、赤谷 K1 等品种，克服了金苗不抗倒伏的弊端，具有产量高、口感佳、颜色黄的优良品种特征。以红谷为材料选育出的丰红谷系列，则克服了红谷产量低的弊端。

敖汉旗采用品种与品牌一起推广的“双推”模式，以敖汉小米品牌促进传统谷子品种推广，用农业文化遗产影响力推广敖汉小米品牌，为敖汉本地培育的谷子品种的推广打下基础，加快了敖汉谷子品种的推广速度。受敖汉小米品牌影响，旗外谷子主产区也选择敖汉谷子品种作为当地主推品种，例如敖汉的黄金苗品种已进入山西、陕西、甘肃等地谷子主产区种植和销售。传统品种还被开发成月子米、石碾米、四色米、金苗米、红谷米、富硒米等系列小米产品，深受市场欢迎。

专家现场指导交流（敖汉旗农牧局 / 提供）
Experts Are Providing Advice and Communicating on the Spot (Provided by AAHB)

Chifeng Agriculture and Animal Husbandry Science Institute has also successfully selected such varieties as Jinmiao K Series and Chigu K1 by taking Jinmiao as the material. These varieties, having overcome the disadvantage that Jinmiao is not lodging resistance, have characteristics of good varieties such as high yield, excellent flavor and dark color. Fenghonggu Series selected by taking Honggu as the material have overcome the disadvantage that the yield of Honggu is low.

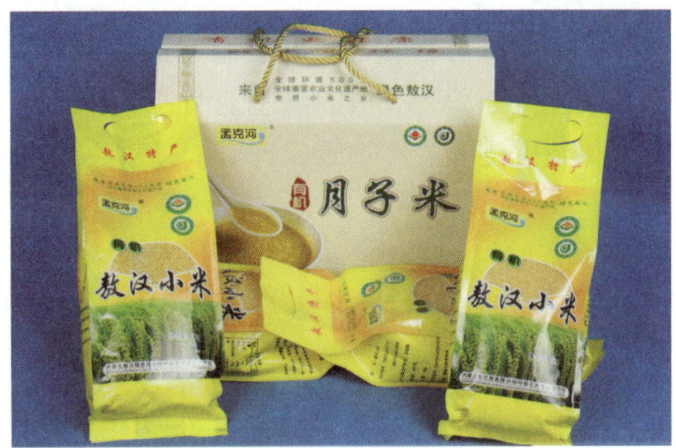

月子米（敖汉旗农牧局 / 提供）
Millet for Puerperal Period (Provided by AAHB)

Based on the "double promotion" model that the variety and the brand are promoted together, Aohan Banner has advanced the promotion of the traditional millet varieties through the brand of Aohan millet. Besides, Aohan Banner promotes the brand of Aohan millet by means of the influence of the agricultural heritage, which has not only laid a foundation for the promotion of the millet variety cultivated in Aohan, but also speeded up the promotion of the millet variety in Aohan Banner. Under the influence of the brand of Aohan millet, millet production areas outside Aohan Banner have also chosen Aohan millet varieties as their main varieties. For example, Huangjinmiao Variety in Aohan has been planted and sold in millet production areas of Shanxi Province, Shaanxi Province and Gansu Province. The millet serial products such as millet for puerperal period, stone roll grinded millet, four-color millet, Jinmiao millet, Honggu millet and Se-rich millet, etc. developed from the traditional varieties are warmly welcomed in the market.

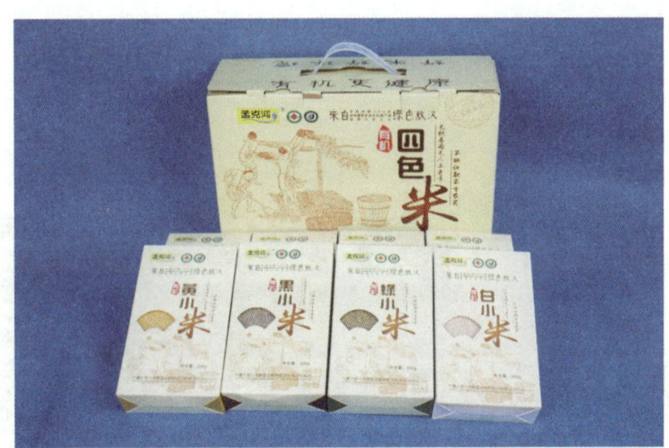

四色米（敖汉旗农牧局 / 提供）
Four-color Millet (Provided by AAHB)

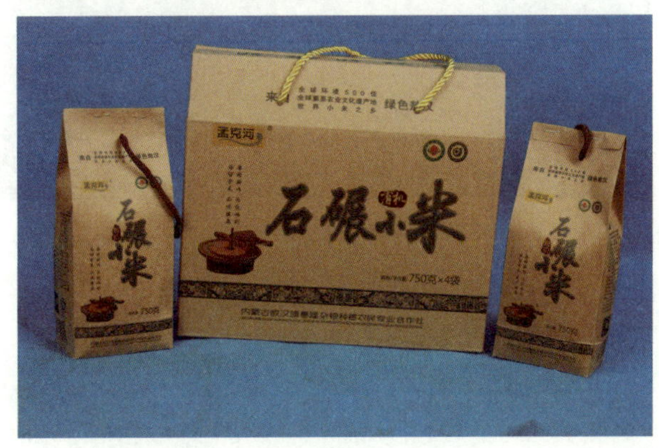

石碾小米（敖汉旗农牧局 / 提供）
Stone Milled Millet (Provided by AAHB)

开展种质资源研究

敖汉旗因具有“世界小米之乡”“全国谷子优质生产基地”“全球重要农业文化遗产”的独特优势，成为开展谷子种质资源研究的重要试验地。例如，敖汉旗承担了东北谷子产业带核心区新品种联合鉴定试验，共引进新品种 17 个。敖汉旗还在兴隆洼村和新惠镇建立面积为 5 亩的试验地两处，开展谷子分期播种试验，为敖汉小米气候品质认证提供数据支撑。经过专家评审，以敖谷 1 号为核心品种的敖汉小米气候品质获评特优等级。

我国东北地区 120 份谷子地方品种和育成品种在敖汉旗进行表型鉴定。结果表明，这些品种在鉴定试验中能够正常成熟，在引进和搜集的 281 份品种资源中脱颖而出，但所占比重不足 50%[①]。这说明敖汉旗有着相对独特的生态气候条件，我国的很多谷子品种不能适应敖汉旗的光温条件。根据 10 个主要表型性状，敖汉旗鉴定试验筛选出了综合性状优良的红谷子、毛毛谷等种质资源。

试验地种植（敖汉旗农牧局 / 提供）
Planting at an Experimental Field (Provided by AAHB)

① 相吉山，徐峰，索良喜，程凯，王艳超，孟海龙，张佳乐，贾斌，王冬雪，刁现民．东北地区谷子地方品种和育成品种表型比较分析．植物遗传资源学报，2018，19（4）：642–656．

Xiang Jishan, Xu Feng, Suo Liangxi, Cheng Kai, Wang Yanchao, Meng Hailong, Zhang Jiale, Jia Bin, Wang Dongxue, Diao Xianmin. Comparative Analysis on the Phenotype of Local Varieties and Improved Vatieties of Millet in Northeast Area. Journal of Plant Genetic Resources, 2018, 19 (4): 642-656.

Carry out Research on Germplasm Resources

Thanks to its unique advantages such as "Home of Millet in the World", "National High Quality Millet Production Base" and "Globally Important Agricultural Heritage Systems", Aohan Banner has become an important experimental area to carry out research on the germplasm resources of millet. For example, Aohan Banner has assumed the joint identification test of new varieties in core areas of the northeast millet industrial belt and introduced 17 new varieties totally. Aohan Banner has also built 2 experimental areas taking up an area of 5 mu in Xinglongwa Village and Xinhui Town to carry out the millet sowing experiment by stages in order to provide data support for the climate quality certification of Aohan millet. After the review of experts, the climate quality of Aohan millet which takes Aogu No.1 as the core variety was evaluated the premium grade.

气候品质认证证书

（敖汉小米）

认证对象：敖汉小米（敖谷1号）
认证编号：QHPZ2018004
认证区域：敖汉旗新惠镇和宝国吐农业试验基地
委托单位：敖汉旗小米产业协会
2018年敖汉小米关键生育期天气气候特征：
出苗-拔节期平均气温：21.4℃
拔节-抽穗期累计降水量：126.5毫米
抽穗-乳熟期最高温度：30.0℃
抽穗-乳熟期气温日较差：16.9℃
生育期≥10℃积温：2971.8℃
生育期日照时数：1167小时
小米生长期内光热资源丰富，水分条件适宜，光热水匹配良好，气象灾害较轻，气候优势明显，有利于优质小米的生产。
认证结论：根据气候条件适宜性和小米品质相关性分析评估，本年度该区域气候品质等级认定为：特优
认证有效期：2018年度
认证单位：内蒙古自治区气候中心

日　期：2019年3月1日

气候品质认证证书（敖汉旗农牧局提供）
Climate Quality Certificate (Provided by AAHB)

The phenotype identification of 120 local varieties and improved varieties of millet from northeast area of China are carried out in Aohan Banner. The result shows that these varieties can become mature normally during the qualification test, standing out among the 281 varieties introduced or collected, but the proportion is less than 50%[1]. It indicates that Aohan Banner has a relatively special ecological and climate conditions and many millet varieties in the country can't adapt to the temperature and photoperiod condition of Aohan Banner. In accordance with 10 main phenotypic characters, the germplasm resources such as Hongguzi and Maomaogu with good comprehensive characters are selected through the qualification test.

敖汉旗还对引进和搜集的 115 份谷子品种进行田间种植鉴定，并对产量及表型性状进行分析。通过将 15 个表型性状归纳为 8 个主要因子，共筛选出 10 个综合评价较高的品种（系）[①]。其中，燕谷 18 的产量最高，铁 8050、公谷 74 号和 14H758 的产量和综合评价均较高。种质资源的研究结果不仅为敖汉旗的谷子生产提供优良品种，而且为谷子优良品种选育提供参考。

新技术的应用在种质资源创新中发挥了重要作用。依托敖汉旗农业文化遗产保护与小米产业发展院士工作站，敖汉旗与中国航天科技集团、中国农业科学院、中国农业大学等单位合作开展以谷子为主的杂粮航天育种。2016 年，敖汉旗的四大类 8 个种子单品搭载天宫二号航天器飞上太空育种。截至 2019 年年底，太空育种已进行了 6 代种子选育，已有敖航谷 1 和敖航谷 2 等进入新品种示范和品种登记阶段。太空育种工程有效利用了敖汉旗传统品种的独特性，有利于培育适应性强、产量高、品质优的农作物品种，促进敖汉旗农业的长足发展。

太空育种试验田（敖汉旗农牧局 / 提供）
Research and Experimental Field for Space Breeding (Provided by AAHB)

① 徐峰，索良喜，孟海龙，李桂红，程凯，张佳乐，贾斌，王冬雪，相吉山. 不同来源谷子品种产量比较及综合评价. 中国农业科技导报，2018，20（5）：100–110.

Xu Feng, Suo Liangxi, Meng Hailong, Li Jiahong, Cheng Kai, Zhang Jiale, Jia Bin, Wang Dongxue, Xiang Jishan. Comparison and Comprehensive Evaluation on the Yield of Millet Varieties with Different Origins. Journal of Agricultural Science and Technology, 2018, 20 (5): 100-110.

太空育种海南试验地（敖汉旗农牧局 / 提供）
Experimental Field for Space Breeding in Hainan island(Provided by AAHB)

Aohan Banner has also appraised 115 millet varieties introduced and collected through the field planting and analyzed their yield and phenotypic characters. By concluding 15 phenotypic characters into 8 main factors, 10 varieties (strains)① with higher comprehensive evaluation are selected totally. Among them, the yield of Yangu 18 is the highest and both the yield and the comprehensive evaluation of Tie 8050, Gonggu No. 74 and 14H758 are high. The research result of the germplasm resources has provided not only high quality varieties for the millet production in Aohan Banner, but also references to the seed selection of high quality millet varieties.

The application of new technology has played an important role in the innovation of germplasm resources. With the help of the academician workstation of agricultural heritage conservation and millet industry development, Aohan Banner has cooperated with the Aerospace Science and Technology Corporation, Chinese Academy of Agricultural Sciences and China Agricultural University to carry out the space mutation breeding of the coarse grain mainly composed of millet. In 2016, four categories with eight seed single items of Aohan Banner were sent for the space breeding by Tiangong-2 spacecraft. As of the end of 2019, seed selections of 6 generations have been sent for space breeding. Aohanggu-1 and Aohanggu-2 have entered the stage of the new variety demonstration and the variety registration. The space breeding engineering has effectively utilized the uniqueness of the traditional varieties in Aohan Banner. It can help to cultivate the crop varieties with strong adaptability, high yield and high quality and promote the sustainable development of the agriculture in Aohan Banner.

CHAPTER 2

第2章

Cooperatives and Production Base Construction

合作社与生产基地建设

惠隆合作社——国家级示范合作社（武文杰 / 摄）
Huilong Cooperative - National Model Cooperative (Taken by Wu Wenjie)

在敖汉旱作农业系统的保护与发展中，农民专业合作社起到了重要作用。为完善敖汉小米产业链条，全旗组建了 366 家种植专业合作社，引进了 27 家龙头企业。2019 年，仅龙头企业、合作社带动年销售敖汉小米就达 1 万吨，直接为全旗农牧民增加收入 2 亿元。其中，敖汉旗惠隆杂粮种植农民专业合作社（以下简称“惠隆合作社”）是全旗种植专业合作社的佼佼者。

惠隆合作社位于敖汉旗新惠镇扎赛营子村，成立于 2008 年 11 月 4 日。十多年的摸索让惠隆合作社的“合作社 + 基地 + 农户”模式日趋成熟，形成了统一种质、统一肥料、统一管理、统一回收、统一加工和统一销售的“六统一”。惠隆合作社于 2013 年被中华全国供销总社评为“全国农民专业合作社示范社”，理事长王国军先生于 2015 年荣获“全球重要农业文化遗产保护与发展贡献奖”，农民社员在合作社的带领下实现了脱贫致富，享受到了农业文化遗产保护与发展的经济效益。

Farmers' specialized cooperatives have played an important role in the conservation and development of Aohan Dryland Farming System. In order to improve the industrial chain of Aohan millet, 366 specialized planting cooperatives have been set up in the whole banner and 27 leading enterprises have been introduced to Aohan Banner. In 2019, only the leading enterprises and the cooperatives have promoted the sales of Aohan millet with 10000 tons, which has increased the income of farmers and herdsmen by RMB 200,000,000 yuan in the banner. Among the cooperatives, Aohan Huilong Coarse Grain Planting Farmers' Specialized Cooperative (hereinafter referred to as "Huilong Cooperative") is the best one of specialized planting cooperatives in the whole banner.

Huilong Cooperative, located at Zhasaiyingzi Village of Xinhui Town, Aohan Banner, was founded on November 4, 2008. More than ten years' development has made its "cooperative+ base+ farmers" model more mature and formed "six uniform aspects" including uniform seeds, uniform manure, uniform management, uniform harvest, uniform processing and uniform sales. Huilong Cooperative was elected as "National Farmers' Specialized Model Cooperative" by All China Federation of Supply and Marketing Cooperatives in 2013. Mr. Wang Guojun, the director-general of the cooperative won "GIAHS Conservation and Development Contribution Award" in 2015. The farmer members have got rid of poverty and become better off under the leadership of the cooperative and shared the welfare brought from the conservation and development of the heritage.

惠隆合作社荣誉（武文杰 / 摄）
Honors of Huilong Cooperative (Taken by Wu Wenjie)

坚持绿色发展理念，保证产品质量

惠隆合作社坚持绿色发展理念，拒绝引入非传统品种种质，严格控制化肥用量，不施用除草剂和农药，以达到绿色产品标准。在此基础上，合作社进一步加强管控，实现了有机生产。2019 年，合作社种植面积共 45 000 亩，其中 15 000 亩实现有机认证，30 000 亩通过绿色产品认证，覆盖扎赛营子村在内的 5 个村。

为保证产品质量，惠隆合作社严守生产标准，在“不定期抽查，违规者退股”的基础上，对农民实行“分组管理、内部监督、连坐问责”的制度，最大程度地保障了产品的“真绿色”和“真有机”。在产品管理上，20 余种杂粮单品在有机认证上达到了“一品一标”，且每个产品都拥有独一无二的“身份证”和追溯码。这些措施不仅规范了农民的生产行为，使有机和绿色生产落到实处，而且为产品走向国内和国际市场提供了保障。

有机（杂粮）种植示范基地（敖汉旗农牧局 / 提供）
Planting Model Base of Organic Coarse Grain (Provided by AAHB)

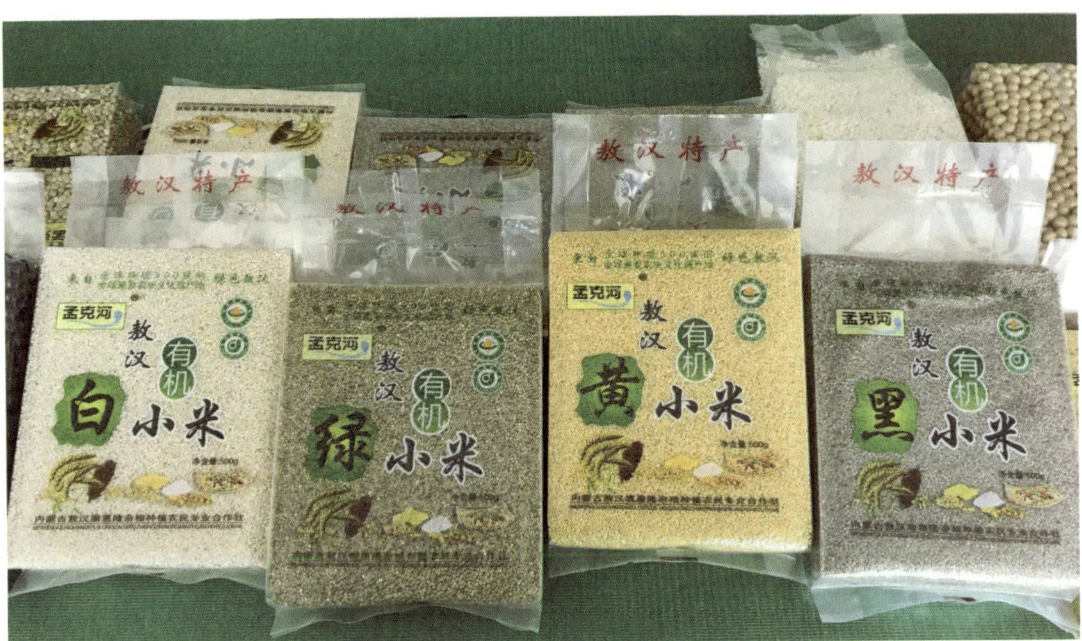

有机四色小米（敖汉旗农牧局 / 提供）
Organic Four-color Millet (Provided by AAHB)

Adhere to the Concept of Green Development and Ensure Product Quality

Huilong Cooperative adheres to the concept of green development, rejects the introduction of the transgenic seeds, strictly controls the dosage of the chemical fertilizer and prohibits the application of herbicides and pesticides in order to meet the green standard. Based on this, the cooperative further enhances its management and control to realize the organic production. In 2019, the planting area of the cooperative took up 45000 mu, of which 15000 mu realized organic certification and 30000 mu passed green certification, covering 5 villages including Zhasaiyingzi Village.

In order to ensure the product quality, Huilong Cooperative strictly adheres to the production standards. Based on the idea that "irregular spot-checking should be applied and those who violate regulations of the cooperative should withdraw their shares", the cooperative adopts the policy of "grouping management, internal supervision, joint accountability" in an effort to ensure, to the full extent, the "real green" and "real organic" products. In terms of the product management, more than 20 items of coarse grains have reached "different standards for different products" concerning the organic certification, and each product has a unique "identity card" and traceability code. These measures have not only normalized farmers' production actions and implemented the green and organic production, but also provided a guarantee for products to enter the domestic and international markets.

依托科技力量，谋求长足发展

在中国农业科学院、中国农业大学、赤峰农业科技研究院、赤峰学院等科研机构的支持下，惠隆合作社在品种优化、产品开发等方面均取得显著成效。在耕地地力调查、秸秆还田推广、绿肥技术更新、肥料配方优化、施肥方法改进等方面，惠隆合作社也得到了敖汉旗农牧局技术服务中心的技术支持。这一系列科技保障工作不仅提高了作物产量、增加了农民收入，还起到了生态环境保护的作用。

为了提高产品的加工质量，惠隆合作社一方面引进河南农太集团、山东昆鸿集团的生产线，实现了加工产品的大量输出，另一方面，从悠久的农耕历史和传统的农耕技艺中获得灵感，引进了多台石碾台。石碾台通过低速低温的碾制使米胚中的活性物质不被破坏，营养不至流失，保留了原汁原味的醇厚口感。得益于此，石碾小米成为招牌产品“月子米”的重要原料，形成了独树一帜的惠隆特色。

惠隆加工设备（敖汉旗农牧局 / 提供）
Processing Facilities of Huilong (Provided by AAHB)

惠隆加工车间（敖汉旗农牧局 / 提供）
Processing Workshops of Huilong (Provided by AAHB)

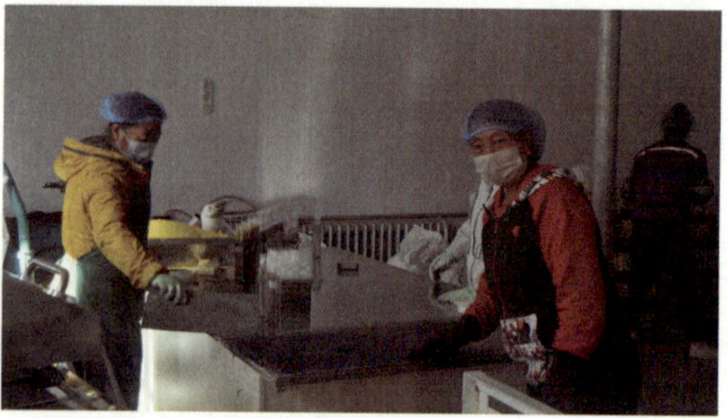

社员在仓库忙碌工作（武文杰 / 摄）
Cooperative Members Were Busy With Their Work (Taken by Wu Wenjie)

In order to ensure the product quality, Huilong Cooperative strictly adheres to the production standards. Based on the idea that "irregular spot-checking should be applied and those who violate regulations of the cooperative should withdraw their shares", the cooperative adopts the policy of "grouping management, internal supervision, joint accountability" in an effort to ensure, to the full extent, the "real green" and "real organic" products. In terms of the product management, more than 20 items of coarse grains have reached "different standards for different products" concerning the organic certification, and each product has a unique "identity card" and traceability code. These measures have not only normalized farmers' production actions and implemented the green and organic production, but also provided a guarantee for products to enter the domestic and international markets.

Depend on Scientific and Technological Support and Seek Sustainable Development

With the support from scientific research institutions such as Chinese Academy of Agricultural Sciences, Chifeng Agricultural Science and Technology Institute, China Agricultural University and Chifeng College, Huilong Cooperative has made a great progress in the variety optimization and the product development. With regard to the farmland productivity investigation, the promotion of returning straw to the field, the technological updating of green manure, the optimization of fertilizer formulation and the improvement of fertilization method, Huilong Cooperative has also acquired the technological support from the Technology Service Center of Agriculture and Animal Husbandry Bureau of Aohan Banner. These series of scientific and technological guarantee measures have not only improved the crop yield and increased farmers' incomes, but also protected the ecological environment.

In order to improve the processing quality of products, Huilong Cooperative, on the one hand, introduced the production lines from Henan Nongtai Group and Shandong Kunhong Group to increase the output of the processed products. On the other hand, Huilong Cooperative acquiring the inspiration from the long agricultural history and the traditional farming skills introduced several millstones. Grinding through millstones at a low speed and temperature retains the active substance and nutrition of the millet germ, which reserves the original mellow taste. Thanks to these production methods, the stone milled millet has become an important raw material of the signature product"millet for puerperal period" and formed a unique characteristic of Huilong.

创新销售模式，拓展销售空间

惠隆合作社在销售上采用农超无缝对接、商店直营为主、淘宝微店为辅的销售模式。通过减少中间环节、增加价格优势，既让产品有口皆碑、远销千里，又让利合作农户，增加农民收入。

为了迎合市场和消费者的需求，惠隆合作社还通过深加工延长产业链，提高产品附加值，拓展销售空间。除了谷子、黍子、高粱、玉米等的初加工之外，合作社目前还加工生产玉米面、荞麦面等产品，并计划利用新建厂房和设备，加工生产速食面条、速食营养粉等上班族所需的健康方便食品。

惠隆合作社还不断推动产品走出国门。惠隆杂粮多次在世界小米起源与发展国际会议、国际有机大米及精品杂粮博览会等国际盛会上亮相。印有“来自全球重要农业文化遗产地”的小米以精美的包装、过硬的品质、合理的价格广受海外朋友赞誉。

苦荞粉（敖汉旗农牧局 / 提供）
Tartarian Buckwheat Flour (Provided by AAHB)

有机荞麦粉（敖汉旗农牧局 / 提供）
Organic Buckwheat Flour (Provided by AAHB)

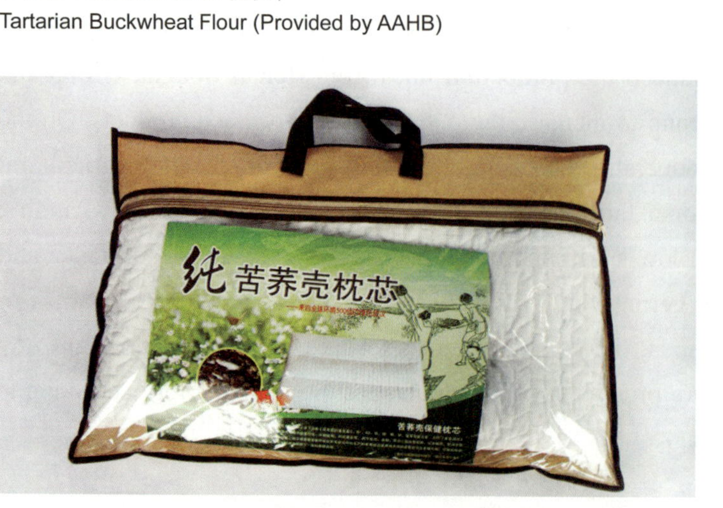

荞麦壳枕（敖汉旗农牧局 / 提供）
Buckwheat Pillow (Provided by AAHB)

Innovate Sales Models and Expand Sales Space

Huilong Cooperative adopts the sales model of seamless farming-supermarket docking and the direct sales of stores as main channels, and the micro shops on Taobao as an auxiliary channel. By means of reducing intermediate links and increasing the price advantage, Huilong Cooperative has not only made its products win universal praise and be sold to thousands of miles away, but also surrendered part of its profits to cooperative farmers to increase their incomes.

In order to meet the requirements of the market and consumers, Huilong Cooperative has increased the added value of products and expanded the sales space by extending the industrial chain through the deep processing. In addition to the pre-processing of the millet, the broomcorn millet, the sorghum and the corn, the cooperative now also produces the corn flour and the buckwheat flour, etc. Besides, the cooperative plans to produce healthy and convenient food such as instant noodles and the instant nutrition powder which are needed by office workers.

“孟克河”小米亮相世博会（敖汉旗农牧局 / 提供）
“Mengkehe” Millet Displayed at World Exposition

Huilong Cooperative also continues to sell its products worldwide. Huilong coarse grain has been displayed in international conferences and exhibitions for several times such as the International Conference on the Origin and Development of the Millet and International Organic Rice and Quality Coarse Grain Exhibition, etc. The millet whose packing bags are printed with words “coming from a GIAHS site” is widely praised by overseas friends thanks to its exquisite package, high quality and reasonable price.

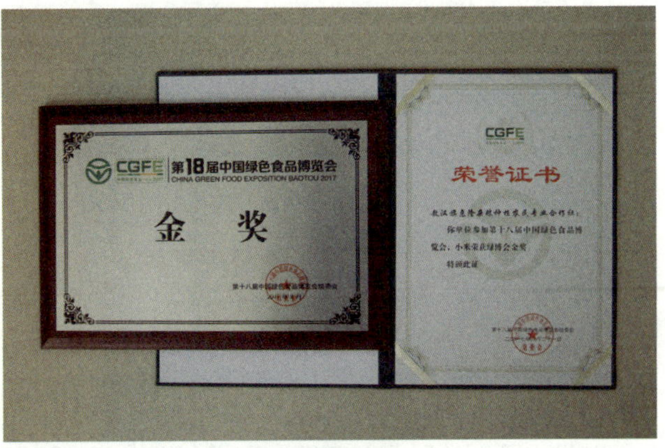

第 18 届绿博会金奖（敖汉旗农牧局 / 提供）
Huilong Cooperative Won the Gold Award of the 18th Green Food Exposition (Provided by AAHB)

实践证明，“合作社 + 基地 + 农户”模式在实现标准化种植、塑造品牌、农户扶贫等方面发挥了重要作用。在管理层面，合作社能够引进先进技术，组织农民培训；在生产层面，合作社能够实现土地资源的合理配置，开展绿色和有机生产，解决产品加工难题；在销售层面，合作社减少中间环节，降低销售费用，成为农户与市场之间的纽带。

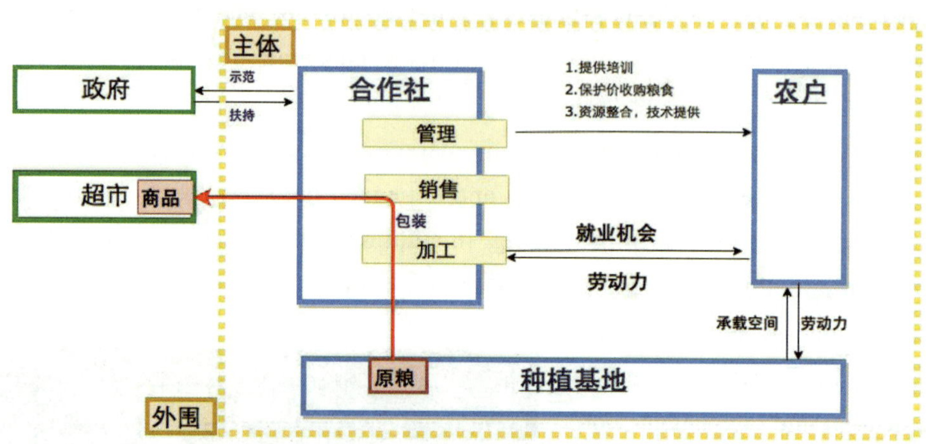

惠隆“合作社 + 基地 + 农户”模式图（敖汉旗农牧局 / 提供）
Huilong's “Cooperative+ Base+ Farmers” Model

在“全球重要农业文化遗产”金字招牌的“加持”下，合作社也以自身示范作用反哺遗产地。生产标准化、技术专业化、管理规范化、农民素质化的合作社已经成为带动遗产地发展的新兴实体，为遗产地的发展带来新的活力。

Practices have proved that the model of “cooperative + base + farmers” has played an important role in implementing the standard planting, building brands and helping farmers to shake off poverty. At the management level, the cooperative can introduce the advanced technologies and train the farmers; at the production level, the cooperative can distribute the land resources more reasonably and implement green and organic production as well as solve processing difficulties of products; at the sales level, the cooperative can reduce the intermediate links and cut down the sales cost as well as link the farmers to the market.

With the help of the honorable GIAHS title, the cooperative also gives its own advantages back to the heritage site. The cooperatives which have standard production, professional techniques, standard management and well-trained farmers have become the emerging entities to lead the development of the heritage site and added new vitality to the development of the heritage site.

CHAPTER 3
第3章

Development of Agricultural Industrialization
农业产业化发展

优质的生产环境、政府的大力扶持、独特的文化品牌效应是遗产地得天独厚的发展优势，而农业产业化则为遗产地的发展带来新契机。在龙头企业的带动下，一家一户的分散生产得到有机联动，形成“小规模、大群体”的格局。农业产业化与遗产地特色相结合，“文化 + 产业”孕育的优势农产品成为主打商品，显著提高其市场竞争力。

为加速农业产业化发展，敖汉旗采取“产品引龙头，政府扶龙头”的策略，通过龙头企业带领农民规避市场风险，规范生产行为，共奔富裕之路。其中，内蒙古金沟农业发展有限公司（以下简称“金沟农业”）“市场牵龙头，龙头带基地，基地连农户”的特色优势作用发挥显著，成为敖汉杂粮企业中的“领头羊”。

截至 2019 年年底，金沟农业有机杂粮种植基地 1.12 万亩，绿色杂粮种植基地 20 万亩，建设完成可容纳 56 万只蛋鸡的标准化养殖场、年产 10 万吨的饲料厂、年产 10 万吨的杂粮加工厂和可容纳 7.50 万吨（1.5 亿斤）粮食的收储库。“兴隆沟”牌小米荣获第十三届、第十六届中国国际农产品交易会参展产品金奖。公司先后成为敖汉小米产业协会会长单位、赤峰农牧业产业化龙头企业协会副会长单位和内蒙古谷子（小米）产业技术创新战略联盟盟主单位。

金沟农业办公楼（敖汉旗农牧局 / 提供）
Jingou Agriculture’s Office Building (Provided by AAHB)

The quality production environment, vigorous support from the government and the brand effect of the heritage are the unique advantages of the heritage site, while the agricultural industrialization brings new opportunity for the development of the heritage site. Under the guidance of the leading enterprises, the previous production which was made by each family separately is now combined together to form a "small-scale but large-group" pattern. The combination between the agricultural industrialization and the heritage characteristics can help the advantageous agricultural products planted in the heritage site become the leading products, which has greatly improved their market competitiveness.

金沟农业获重点龙头企业称号（敖汉旗农牧局 / 提供）
Jingou Agriculture Acquired the Title of "Important Leading Enterprise" (Provided by AAHB)

Agricultural Development Co., Ltd. (hereinafter referred to as "Jingou Agriculture") has made full use of the advantage that "the market guides the production of the leading enterprises, and the leading enterprises lead the production base, which links the farmers" and become the "leader" of coarse grain enterprises in Aohan.

As of the end of 2019, Jingou Agriculture has 11200 mu of the organic coarse grain planting base, 200000 mu of the green coarse grain planting base, a standardized farm holding 560000 laying hens, a feed mill with a capacity of 100000 tons of fodder annually, a coarse grain processing factory with a capacity of 100000 tons annually and a storage center with a capacity of 75900 tons (150,000,000 jin①) of grains. The "Xinglonggou" brand millet won gold awards of all exhibition products at the 13th China International Agricultural Trade Fair and the 16th China International Agricultural Trade Fair. The company has become the chairman company of Aohan Millet Industrial Association, the vice-chairman company of Leading Enterprises Association of Chifeng Agricultural and Animal Husbandry Industrialization and the chairman company of Inner Mongolia Millet Industrial and Technological Innovation Strategic Alliances successively.

"兴隆沟"有机小米获农产品金奖（敖汉旗农牧局 / 提供）
"Xinglonggou" Organic Millet Won Gold Award of Agricultural Products (Provided by AAHB)

① 1 jin = 500 g

“公司 + 合作社 + 农户”管理体系

金沟农业采取“公司 + 合作社 + 农户”的管理体系。其合作社属公司领办型合作社，是农民和公司沟通的桥梁。农户在自家土地上生产，合作社在公司的生产计划和物资支持下，与农民签订种植协议，统一调配种子、分发有机肥、提供技术支持，在生产期间进行监督，并提供信息及技术咨询服务等，以确保绿色有机，对于产品，公司再以高于市场价格进行回收。

“产前供种、产中供肥、产后收购，统一扣费”的一条龙模式为农民提供一站式支持。企业没有大包大揽全机械化种植，而是保留了传统的耕作模式，同时采用贴心的服务措施减轻了农民生产过程中的负担，为产品质量稳定提供了强有力的后盾。

小米加工生产线（敖汉旗农牧局 / 提供）
Production Line of Millet Processing (Provided by AAHB)

现代化鸡舍（敖汉旗农牧局 / 提供）
Modern Chicken House (Provided by AAHB)

全产业链循环农业模式

金沟农业实行全产业链循环农业模式，通过“两个基地，一个园区”的布局实现了生产过程的“物尽其用”。种植基地是粮食种植的主阵地；养殖基地以蛋鸡养殖场为中心，饲料加工厂和有机肥厂为辅助；加工园区则集粮食收储、杂粮初加工、杂粮鸡蛋精深加工为一体。

种植基地产出的原粮在园区进行加工，初级加工的粮食是核心销售产品，而精深加工的蛋卷及杂粮饼干则是延伸产品，二者经公司销售系统进入市场。粮食加工过程中剩余的秸秆谷壳将输入养殖基地，作为饲料加工的原材料。蛋鸡养殖过程产生的粪便在收集后进入有机肥厂进行发酵，制成鸡粪农家肥，再由合作社分发给农民用于杂粮种植，回归种植基地，从而实现了全产业链循环。

"Company + Cooperative + Farmers" Management System

Jingou Agriculture adopts the management system of "company+ cooperative+ farmers". Its cooperative belongs to the company-leading cooperative which is also a bridge of communication between farmers and the company. Farmers produce grains on their own lands while the cooperative signs a planting agreement with farmers under the production plan of the company and provides material and fund support for these farmers. Then, the company will distribute seeds uniformly, hand out the organic fertilizer and provide the technical support for farmers. During the production period, the company will supervise farmers' production in order to ensure the green and organic products and provide information and technical consulting services for farmers, etc. Next, the company will buy products from farmers at a price higher than the market price.

The one-stop mode of "seed supply before production, manure supply during the production, purchase after the production and uniform fee deduction" provides one-stop support for farmers. The company keeps traditional planting methods instead of adopting mechanized planting completely. The thoughtful service provided by the company has eased farmers' burden during the production and provided powerful support for them.

Circular Agriculture Model of Whole Industrial Chain

Jingou Agriculture adopts the circular agriculture model of the whole industrial chain. The layout of "two bases and one industrial park" makes full use of everything during the production. In the breeding base, the laying hen farm is the center while the feed mill and the organic fertilizer factory is auxiliary; the planting base is the main area of the grain planting; the processing industrial park integrates the grain storage, the preliminary processing of the coarse grain, the intensive and deep processing of the coarse grain and eggs.

The unprocessed grain produced from the production base will be processed in the industrial park. The grain after priliminary processing is the major sales product while the egg rolls and the cereals biscuits after the intensive and deep processing are the augmented products. Both of them enter the market through the sales system of the company. The straw and chaff which are not used during the grain processing will be brought to the breeding base as the raw material of the feed processing. The feces produced during the laying hen breeding will be collected and transformed into the chicken manure after the fermentation at the organic fertilizer factory. Then, the cooperative will hand it out to farmers for the coarse grain planting at the planting base. In this way, the circulation of the whole industrial chain is realized.

四通八达的销售系统

在销售上，金沟农业广拓途径，多渠并重。公司与各大商超无缝对接，产品通过自营物流渠道直达商超。目前，“兴隆沟”牌杂粮已成功入驻物美、大润发、乐天百货等大型连锁商超，并在华南、华北、西北等区域建立起经销网络，走进千家万户。公司还与各大餐饮企业积极对接，为嘉和一品等集团源源不断地输入杂粮原料。公司还利用电商信息传递快、中间环节少、人力成本低、企业宣传强的优势，在天猫、京东、苏宁易购等线上平台建立品牌销售旗舰店。

“兴隆沟”产品在小米大会进行场外展示（敖汉旗农牧局 / 提供）

Off-site Display of “Xinglonggou” Products duringg the Millet Conference (Provided by AAHB)

“兴隆沟”系列产品（敖汉旗农牧局 / 提供）

“Xinglonggou” Serial Products (Provided by AAHB)

未来几年，金沟农业将在国内形成以北京、上海、广东、深圳等地为核心，辐射全国大中城市的高效农产品供应网络，以电商、超市、特供、专营店、经销商为 5 个支点，整合线上线下销售渠道，为客户提供全程“一站式”服务，集中力量打造农业品牌。

金沟农业始终坚持全产业链循环农业模式，并与深圳市百绿生物染色体杂交研究所、中国农业大学、内蒙古农业大学等院校和科研机构实行产、学、研合作，通过观念创新、产品创新、技术创新和管理创新，实现公司可持续快速发展。同时，公司积极发挥敖汉作为“世界小米之乡”“旱作农业发源地”“优质杂粮产地”的地域优势，依托“全球环境 500 佳”“全球重要农业文化遗产地”两个世界品牌，做大杂粮产业。公司所形成的“管理—生产—销售”模式对遗产地农业产业化发展具有重要借鉴意义。

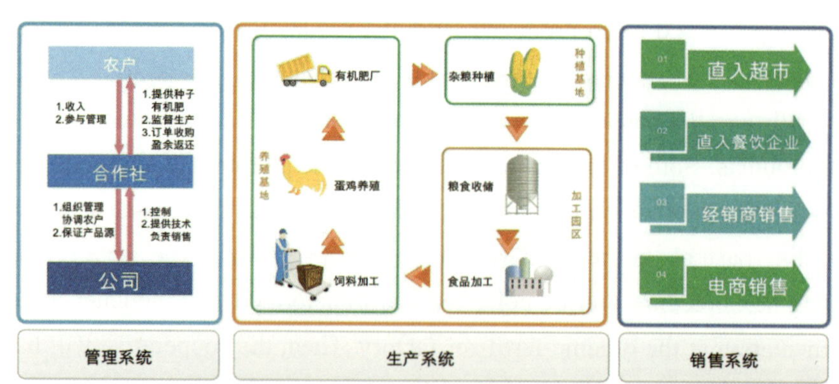

金沟农业的“管理 - 生产 - 销售”模式示意图（敖汉旗农牧局 / 提供）

The “Management - Production - Sales” Model of Jingou Agriculture (Provided by AAHB)

All-round Sales System

In terms of the sales, Jingou Agriculture expands its sales channels. The company has realized the seamless connection with major supermarkets and its products are directly sold in these supermarkets through its logistics group. "Xinglonggou" brand coarse grain has been successfully sold in large supermarkets such as Wu Mart, RT-MART and LOTTE Department Store, etc. Jingou Agriculture has also established its distribution network in southern, northern and northwestern areas of China in an effort to make its products enjoyed by thousands of households. Besides, the company has also cooperated with large catering enterprises actively. For example, the company delivers its coarse grains to Jiaheyipin Group continuously. The company has also established its brand sales flagship store online on platforms such as Tmall, JD.com and suning.com because of advantages of e-commerce platforms such as the fast communication speed, few intermediate links, low cost of labor forces and favorable company promotion.

The company plans to form a core efficient agricultural product supply network in Beijing, Shanghai, Guangdong and Shenzhen to promote its sales in large and medium-sized cities in the country in next few years. The company will integrate its online and offline sales channels through five channels such as the e-commerce, supermarket, special supply, franchise stores and the distributor in an effort to provide an all-round "one-stop" service for its customers and focus on building an agricultural brand.

Jingou Agriculture always adheres to the circular agriculture model of the whole industrial chain, and makes the industrial-academic-research cooperation with universities and scientific research institutes such as Shenzhen Bailv Biological Chromosome Hybridization Institute, China Agricultural University and Inner Mongolia Agricultural University. The company has realized a sustainable and rapid development by means of the idea innovation, product innovation, technical innovation and management innovation. At the same time, the company has strengthened its coarse grain industry by actively giving play to the regional advantage of Aohan as "Home of Millet in thc World", "Origin Area of Dryland Farming" and "Quality Coarse Grain Production Place", and depending on two world famous brands such as "Global 500 Roll of Honour for Environment Achievement" and "Globally Important Agricultural Heritage Systems". The model of "management- production - sales" formed by the company can provide an important reference to the agricultural industrialization development of the heritage site.

CHAPTER 4

第4章

Development of Cultural Products

文化产品开发

微电影，深传播

《谷乡之恋》开机仪式（敖汉旗农牧局 / 提供）
Launching Ceremony of *Home of Millet* (Provided by AAHB)

2017 年 1 月，敖汉旗农牧局、赤峰微电影制作中心乘借新媒体东风，以一部微电影《谷乡之恋》，将敖汉旗“华夏第一村”的史前文明、“全球环境 500 佳”的生态文明、“全球重要农业文化遗产”的农耕文明带向公众视野。该片由中国工程院院士李文华先生题写片名，是中国第一部以农业文化遗产为题材的微电影，荣获第五届亚洲微电影艺术节“金海棠奖”，在“中国梦 · 扶贫攻坚影像盛典”颁奖会上脱颖而出，荣获剧情类三等奖，获得 2018 年赤峰市“五个一工程”优秀作品奖。

该片以敖汉返乡创业青年国秀玲为原型，讲述了农家女发展有机农业，带领村民走向富裕之路的故事。片子以农业文化遗产保护与传承为主线，以感情纠葛为铺垫，在中国谷乡敖汉旗演绎了一场加强农业文化遗产传承与保护、带领乡亲共同致富的创业史。正如片名《谷乡之恋》一样，电影诠释着人与人之间的爱恋、人与土地之间的眷恋、人与谷乡农产品之间的依恋。

《谷乡之恋》DVD 照片（敖汉旗农牧局 / 提供）
DVD Photos of *Home of Millet* (Provided by AAHB)

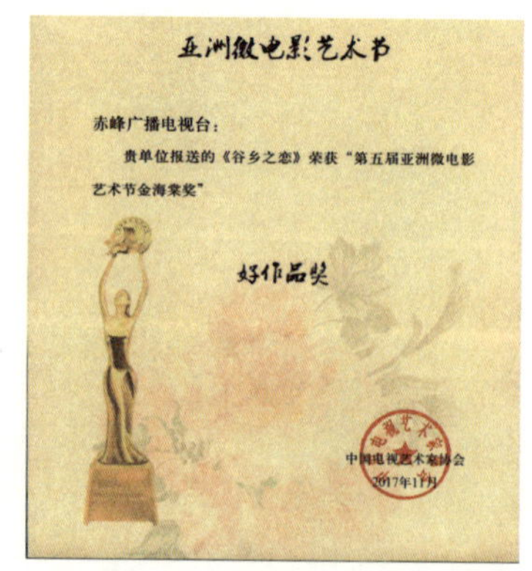
亚洲微电影艺术节

赤峰广播电视台：

贵单位报送的《谷乡之恋》荣获“第五届亚洲微电影艺术节金海棠奖”

好作品奖

中国电视艺术家协会

2017年11月

《谷乡之恋》获金海棠奖（敖汉旗农牧局 / 提供）
Home of Millet Won Golden Begonia Award (Provided by AAHB)

Microfilm with Wide Spread

获奖证书

敖汉旗农业局：

您创作的作品《谷乡之恋》荣获中国梦・扶贫攻坚影像盛典剧情类三等奖。

中国梦・扶贫攻坚影像盛典组委会
二〇一八年五月二十六日

《谷乡之恋》获奖证书（敖汉旗农牧局 / 提供）
Certificates of Awards & Honors of *Home of Millet* (Provided by AAHB)

In January 2017, Agriculture and Animal Husbandry Bureau of Aohan Banner and Chifeng Microfilm Production Center released the microfilm titled Home of Millet, through which the prehistoric civilization of Aohan Banner as "First Village of Ancient China", the ecological civilization of Aohan Banner as "Global 500 Roll of Honour for Environment Achievement" and the farming civilization of Aohan Banner with "Globally Important Agricultural Heritage Systems" were introduced to the public. The name of the film was written by Mr. Li Wenhua, an academician of Chinese Academy of Engineering. As the first microfilm about the agricultural heritage system, the film won the "Golden Begonia Award" at The 5th Asia Microfilm Art Festival, stood out and was awarded the Third Prize of all dramatic films at the awarding ceremony of "The Chinese Dream.Poverty Alleviation Film Ceremony", and the Outstanding Work Prize of "Five One Project (a good book, a good TV series, a good play, a good film, a good article)" in Chifeng City in 2018.

The film is based on the story of Guo Xiuling, a young entrepreneur returning hometown from cities. The story is that Guo Ling, a farmer's daughter, leads villagers to become rich by means of the development of the organic agriculture. The film focuses on the conservation and inheritance of the agricultural heritage system and develops by the emotional entanglement. It mainly tells about the history of entrepreneurship in the home of millet - Aohan Banner, to strengthen the inheritance and conservation of the agricultural heritage and lead fellow villagers to shake off poverty. Just as the name of the film *Home of Millet* indicates, the film tells about the love among people, people's attachment to the land and people's enthusiasm to the agricultural products made in the home of the millet.

《谷乡之恋》人物原型国秀玲（武文杰 / 摄）
Guo Xiuling, the Prototype of Character of *Home of Millet* (Taken by Wu Wenjie)

《谷乡之恋》故事梗概

在外小有成就的女青年郭玲返乡创业，依托农业文化遗产品牌，发展建设以特色种植、养殖于一体的家庭农场和生态农庄，着力生产有机生态食品，打造从田间到餐桌的有机绿色直供通道，发展观光农业和休闲农业，并在老同学、大学生村官薛溢的支持与鼓励下，成功打造出第一个以农业文化遗产为主题的样板餐厅“一村乡土铁锅宴”，生意火爆。郭玲的成功鼓励了当地农民从农业文化遗产的保护与传承中获得经济收入，促进了农业文化遗产保护工作的开展。

《谷乡之恋》对敖汉旗具有重要的意义。它向世界点亮了敖汉 8 000 年粟作历史的名片，是弘扬农业文化遗产的全新举措。该片已通过第四届东亚地区农业文化遗产研讨会、第四届联合国粮食及农业组织农业文化遗产高级别培训班等向亚洲、欧洲、非洲等 27 个国家推介。它将“全球重要农业文化遗产”的荣誉化作植根人们心中的自豪感和认同感，更鼓励了敖汉当地的青年回乡创业。继小米主题餐厅创办后，敖汉拨面馆等与农业文化有关的餐厅也渐渐多了起来，农业文化遗产的保护与传承的队伍正在不断发展扩大。

微电影具有制作成本低廉、剪辑加工简单、传播渠道广泛的优势，是当今社会文化传播的重要途径。利用微电影展现遗产景观、诠释遗产内涵、涵盖遗产作用、科普遗产保护，对农业文化遗产的宣传、保护和发展具有重要作用。敖汉旗在这一领域的探索为其他农业文化遗产地提供了宝贵的借鉴经验。

一片金黄（敖汉旗农牧局 / 提供）
Golden Millet (Provided by AAHB)

Synopsis of *Home of Millet*

Guo Ling, a young girl who has been successful in cities previously, returns to her hometown to start a new business. In consideration of the agricultural heritage brand at her hometown, Guo Ling determines to build an ecological family farm which integrates the characteristic crop-planting and breeding industry. Guo Ling aims to produce organic and ecological food, build a direct delivery channel of the organic and green agricultural products from the farmland to the dining table, and develop sightseeing agriculture and leisure agriculture. With the support and encouragement of Xue Yi who is her old classmate and works as a college-graduate village official, Guo Ling succeeds in creating the first theme restaurant of agricultural heritage named "Delicious Countryside Food", which is very popular. The success of Guo Ling has encouraged local farmers to acquire economic incomes from the conservation and inheritance of the agricultural heritage system and promoted its conservation.

Home of Millet is very significant for Aohan Banner. The film has introduced the 8000-year-long millet planting history of Aohan to the world and is a new measure to carry forward the agricultural heritage system. The film has been introduced to the representatives from 27 countries in Asia, Europe and Africa through the 4th Conference of the East Asia Research Association for Agricultural Heritage Systems and the 4th FAO High-level Training Class on Agricultural Heritage Systems. The film has transformed the honor of "Globally Important Agricultural Heritage Systems" into local people's sense of pride and sense of identity, which has encouraged local young people to return to their hometown to start a new business in turn. After the millet themed restaurant is created, more restaurants related to the agriculture such as Aohan Bomiao Restaurant are also opened, which has encouraged more people to participate in the conservation and inheritance of the agricultural heritage system.

Microfilm has advantages such as low cost, simple editing and processing, and wide communication channels, so it has become an important way of the cultural communication in modern society. The microfilm plays an important role in the promotion, conservation and development of the agricultural heritage systems in that it can show the heritage landscape, explain the heritage connotation, cover the heritage function and publicize the heritage conservation scientifically. The exploration made by Aohan Banner in this field has provided a valuable reference for other agricultural heritage sites.

小故事，大智慧

为了提高农业文化遗产的社会认知度、吸引小朋友及家长去了解农业文化遗产知识，中国科学院地理科学与资源研究所副研究员焦雯珺和北京联合大学旅游学院教授孙业红做了一个大胆的尝试，即采用国际流行的图画绘本方式，通过娓娓道来的童话故事，向小朋友们阐释农业文化遗产的价值精髓。

GIAHS 故事绘本第一辑（焦雯珺 / 摄）
First Set of Picture Books on GIAHS
(Taken by Jiao Wenjun)

第一套全球重要农业文化遗产故事绘本于 2018 年 11 月正式出版。作者创作了“珍惜友谊”“勇于探索”“美的真谛”和“懂得感恩”4 个主题故事，阐释了“浙江青田稻鱼共生系统”“云南红河哈尼稻作梯田系统”“河北宣化城市传统葡萄园”和“福建福州茉莉花与茶文化系统”4 个全球重要农业文化遗产的核心价值。

2019 年 9 月，第五本全球重要农业文化遗产故事绘本面世了，它就是《小米王国的继承人》。这是为敖汉旱作农业系统专门创作的童话故事，故事的主题是“善于思考”。小朋友们可以跟随“黄小米”一起去田野里仔细观察并认真思考，领略敖汉旱作农业系统的价值特点。

《小米王国的继承人》绘本封面（焦雯珺 / 摄）
Cover of the Picture Book Titled Successor *of Millet Kingdom*
(Taken by Jiao Wenjun)

Little Story, Great Wisdom

In order to improve the social awareness of the agricultural heritage systems and attract children and their parents to learn the knowledge about the agricultural heritage systems, Jiao Wenjun, an associate professor of Institute of Geographic Sciences and Natural Resources Research, Chinese Academy of Sciences and Sun Yehong, a professor of Tourism College at Beijing Union University had a bold try. They decided to explain the values and essences of the agricultural heritage systems to children through the way in which they tell a fairy tale slowly by means of picture books which are very popular in the world.

The first set of picture books about the Globally Important Agricultural Heritage Systems was published in November 2018 officially. The authors have created four theme stories including "Cherish Friendship", "Dare to Explore", "Essence of Beauty" and "Be Grateful", and explained the core values of four Globally Important Agricultural heritage Systems such as "Rice-fish Culture in Qingtian, Zhejiang Province", "Hani Rice Terrace System in Honghe, Yunnan Province", "Xuanhua Traditional Vineyard System of Hebei Province" and "Jasmine and Tea Culture System in Fuzhou, Fujian Province".

In September 2019, the fifth picture book on Globally Important Agricultural Heritage Systems was published. It *was Successor of Millet Kingdom*. The fairy story was specially created for Aohan Dryland Farming System themed "being good at thinking". Children can follow "Yellow Millet" to observe the fields carefully and think them about seriously and appreciate the values and characteristics of Aohan Dryland Farming System.

《小米王国的继承人》故事梗概

小米王国的国王日渐年迈，想在 4 个孩子当中挑选 1 位作为继承人。他向孩子们提出一个问题，“这片土地上最宝贵的东西是什么”，并给孩子们一年的时间去寻找答案。谁的答案最让他满意，谁就能成为下一任国王。一年的时间到了，孩子们给出答案。黑小米的答案是美丽的宝石，绿小米的答案是独特的菜肴，白小米的答案是悠久的历史，黄小米的答案是“我们”。黄小米的答案来自田野，是他仔细观察、认真思考得到的。“我们”则是小米王国的所有成员，不仅有小米，还有玉米、高粱米、荞麦米、大黄米、绿豆、红小豆等。正是“我们”让这片土地美丽如画、充满希望。黄小米的答案最让国王满意，自然就成为了下一任国王。

全球重要农业文化遗产故事绘本之《小米王国的继承人》由中国科学院地理科学与资源研究所自然与文化遗产研究中心与敖汉旗人民政府共同策划，并得到了农业农村部国际合作司、中国农学会农业文化遗产分会和中国生态学学会科普工作委员会的联合支持。绘本于 2019 年 9 月举行的第六届世界小米起源与发展会议上正式发行，得到了与会人员的强烈反响和一致好评。

全球重要农业文化遗产故事绘本不仅可以让小朋友们更加深入地了解农业文化遗产的价值精髓，而且可以让小朋友们对中国的农耕文化产生更多的兴趣和认识，更好地感受中国人民勤劳、勇敢、聪慧、仁爱的优秀品质，汲取天人合一、与大自然和谐共生的中华农耕智慧。正如中国科学院地理科学与资源研究所闵庆文研究员所评价的一样，“不仅开辟了农业文化遗产科学普及的一个新领域，更为孩子们了解我国优秀农耕文化打开了一扇新窗户”。

Synopsis of *Successor of Millet Kingdom*

When the king of the millet kingdom becomes old, he plans to choose a successor from his four children. He asks his children a question. "What's the most valuable thing on this land?" He left one year for his children to find out the answer. The one whose answer satisfies him best can be the next king. When one-year time is up, children give their answers to their father. Black Millet answers it is the beautiful gem, while Green Millet answers it is the special dishes. The answer of White Millet is the long history, and Yellow Millet answers "we". Yellow Millet's answer comes from the fields that he observes carefully and thinks about seriously. "We" refers to all members of the millet kingdom, including not only the millet, but also the corn, the sorghum, the buckwheat, the broomcorn millet, the mung bean and the red bean, etc. It is "we" that makes this land picturesque and hopeful. Yellow Millet's answer satisfies the king best, so he becomes the next king naturally.

Successor of Millet Kingdom, as one of picture books about GIAHS, was jointly planned by Center for Natural and Cultural Heritage, Institute of Geographic Sciences and Natural Resources Research, Chinese Academic of Sciences and Aohan Banner People's Government. The creation of the book was supported jointly by Department of International Cooperation, Ministry of Agriculture and Rural Affairs of the People's Republic of China, Agricultural Heritage Systems Branch of China Association of Agricultural Science Societies and Science Popularization Committee of Ecological Society of China. The picture book was officially released at the 6th International Conference on Origin and Development of the Millet held in September 2019. The book acquired strong reactions and was praised by the participants of the conference.

The picture books about GIAHS can not only help children learn about the values and essences of the agricultural heritage systems, but also arouse children's interest in the farming culture of China. Through these books, children can appreciate Chinese people's industrious, courageous, intelligent and humane characters, and learn about Chinese farming wisdom that focuses on the harmony between human and nature and the harmonious coexistence with the nature. Just as Prof. Min Qingwen of Institute of Geographic Sciences and Natural Resources Research, CAS, evaluated that "the picture books not only launch a new field for the science popularization of agricultural heritage systems, but also open a new window for children to learn about the excellent farming culture of our country".

CHAPTER 5
第 5 章

Development of Sustainable Tourism
可持续旅游开发

祈雨祭祖，打造特色旅游品牌

祈雨活动是敖汉地区传承已久的民俗活动。为保护与传承这项民俗活动，自 2013 年起，每年“红山文化陶塑人像”出土纪念日（5 月 23 日），敖汉旗都在位于兴隆洼镇的兴隆沟遗址举办祈雨祭祖活动。这项民俗活动也入选了农业农村部全国 100 个乡村文化活动名单。

兴隆洼祈雨活动有数百人参与，规模大、场面壮观。人们通过朝拜祭祀，祈祷“一季风雨顺、百里粟黍香”“万事如意、幸福安康”。活动因传承旱作农耕文化特色鲜明，吸引了当地老百姓及周边地区的游客前来参观，逐渐成为敖汉旗一项独具特色且富有吸引力的文化旅游活动品牌。

每次祈雨祭祖活动持续 3 天。期间，评剧、皮影戏等传统节目穿插上演，精彩纷呈，村民手工制作的剪纸、柳编等敖汉特色工艺品也颇受欢迎。这些年来，旅游人数和旅游收入均呈现出持续增长，有效带动了兴隆洼镇乃至整个敖汉旗文化旅游产业的发展。

祈雨祭祖仪式（敖汉旗文化旅游局 / 提供）

Beginning of Rain-praying and Ancestor Worship Activity (Provided by Culture and Tourism Bureau of Aohan Banner)

祈雨祭祖活动现场（敖汉旗文化旅游局/提供）
The Scene of Rain-praying and Ancestor Worship Activity (Provided by Culture and Tourism Bureau of Aohan Banner)

Build Special Tourism Brand through Rain-praying and Ancestor Worship

The rain-praying activity is a kind of folk activities inherited for a long time in Aohan area. In order to conserve and inherit this folk activity, Aohan Banner holds rain-praying and ancestor worship activity at Xinglonggou Site in Xinglongwa Town every year on the anniversary (May 23rd) when “pottery figures of Hongshan culture” was unearthed since 2013. The folk activity is also elected into the List of National 100 Rural Cultural Activities by Ministry of Agriculture and Rural Affairs of the People’s Republic of China.

The rain-praying activity in Xinglongwat is large scale and spectacular with hundreds of participants. People pray “good weather for the crop harvest” and “everything to go well and people to have great happiness” through the rain-praying and ancestor worship activity. Due to its distinctive characteristics and inheritance of the dryland farming culture, the activity has attracted local people and tourists coming from surrounding areas. It has gradually become a unique and attractive culture tourism brand of Aohan Banner.

Each rain-praying and ancestor worship activity lasts for three days. During the activity, the wonderful conventional programs such as Pingju Opera and the shadow play are also performed, and the typical handicrafts with Aohan’s characteristics such as paper cuttings and wickerwork made by villagers manually are also very popular. During these years, both the tourist number and the tourist income are increasing, which has effectively promoted the development of the cultural tourism industry of Xinglongwa Town or even the whole Aohan Banner.

小米音乐会，旅游新名片

第一届敖汉小米音乐会（敖汉旗农牧局 / 提供）
The 1st Aohan Millet Concert (Provided by AAHB)

2018 年夏天，敖汉旗举办了一场特殊的音乐会——第一届敖汉小米音乐会，其成为敖汉旗农业文化遗产保护和旅游发展的新名片。

2018 年 6 月，刘海庆带领合作社策划了“第一届敖汉小米音乐会暨敖汉旱作故事全球重要农业文化遗产分享会”。通过微信公众平台对外发布了“这个夏天，寻 3 000 个伙伴，在世界小米之乡办一场音乐会”的众筹号召。2018 年 8 月 18 日，“第一届敖汉小米音乐会暨敖汉旱作故事全球重要农业文化遗产分享会”在敖汉旗兴隆洼镇嘎岔村顺利举行。来自嘎岔村的村干部、合作社的社员和内蒙古大学学生以及在场的观众们分享了农业文化遗产保护背后的故事。专业的民谣乐队和村民一起歌唱世界小米之乡，在音乐中将农业文化遗产讲述给观众，增强公众对农业文化遗产的认知。

音乐会吸引了来自全国各地的观众，不仅观看了精彩节目，还品尝了敖汉拨面、小米饭等当地特色美食，多方位感受农耕文化的魅力。在音乐会的系列活动——畅游遗产地环节，观众们来到中华祖神的出土地。站在世界小米发源地的土地上，感受历经 8 000 年风雨的农耕文化，让他们对于“世界小米之乡”和农业文化遗产都有了更深的认识和了解。

小米音乐会现场（敖汉旗农牧局 / 提供）
The Scene of Millet Concert (Provided by AAHB)

畅游兴隆洼遗址
（敖汉旗农牧局 / 提供）
Visiting Xinglongwa Site
(Provided by AAHB)

Millet Concert, a New Tourism Card

In the summer of 2018, Aohan Banner held a special concert - the 1st Aohan Millet Concert. It has become a new card of the agricultural heritage system conservation and the tourism development of Aohan Banner.

In June 2018, Liu Haiqing led the cooperative members to plan "The 1st Aohan Millet Concert and The Sharing Session on Aohan Dryland Farming Story about GIAHS". He issued a crowdfunding proposal that "3000 partners are needed this summer to hold a concert at the home of the millet in the world" through WeChat public platform. On August 18, 2018, "The 1st Aohan Millet Concert and The Sharing Session on Aohan Dryland Farming Story about GIAHS" was successfully held at Gacha Village, Xinglongwa Town, Aohan Banner. Village cadres from Gacha Village, members of cooperatives, students from Inner Mongolia University and audiences present at the concert shared their stories on the conservation of the agricultural heritage system. Professional folk bands sang for the home of the millet in the world together with villagers. The agricultural heritage system was told to audiences through the music, which strengthened audiences' knowledge about the agricultural heritage system.

The concert attracted audiences from all over the country. They not only watched the wonderful performances, but also tasted local delicacies such as Aohan Bomian and the cooked millet and appreciated the charm of the farming culture from many aspects. During a serial activity of the concert - traveling at the heritage site, audiences visited the birthplace of Chinese ancestral god. When audiences stood on the land of the origin area of the millet in the world and appreciated the 8000-year-long farming culture, they acquired more knowledge and deepened their understanding about the "Home of Millet in the World" and the agricultural heritage system.

农业文化遗产主题餐厅

农业和旅游的融合式发展也在敖汉旗得到体现。敖汉旗打造了以本地为核心、面向东北、覆盖蒙东辽西地区的谷子产业区，还建设了中国小米博物馆、旱作农业主题公园、世界谷种研发基地，创办了农业文化遗产主题餐厅、小米饭农家院，开发了小米旅游产品。敖汉旗已成为享誉塞外的康养圣地。

在农业文化遗产主题餐厅，一进门就能看到敖汉特有的农业文化符号——传统生产工具。石碾子、犁杖、撮子等向人们讲述着一粒小米从田间到的饭桌的过程。餐厅经营小米排骨、小米锅巴等敖汉小米特色美食，深受旅游者欢迎，不少食客专门从外地来到敖汉品一品敖汉的特色美食。

小米美食（敖汉旗农牧局 / 提供）
Millet Food (Provided by AAHB)

这家主题餐厅的创办人国秀玲，便是微电影《谷乡之恋》中女主角郭玲的原型人物。为了保护农业文化遗产，也为了传承记忆中的家乡味道，2015 年国秀玲返乡创业，在敖汉开了这家餐厅。依托农业文化遗产品牌，通过发展建设特色种植、养殖于一体的家庭农场和生态农庄，着力生产有机生态食品，打造田间到餐桌的有机绿色直供通道，发展观光农业和休闲农业，国秀玲成功打造出第一个以农业文化遗产为主题的样板餐厅——一村乡土铁锅宴。国秀玲的成功不仅启发了当地农民如何从农业文化遗产的保护与传承中受益，也为当地开创了农业和旅游融合式发展的新路径。

农业文化遗产主题餐厅（敖汉旗农牧局 / 提供）
Agricultural Heritage Theme Restaurant (Provided by AAHB)

Agricultural Heritage Theme Restaurant

The integrated development of agriculture and tourism can be also seen in Aohan Banner. Aohan Banner has established a millet industrial area which focuses on Aohan Banner, faces the northeastern area of China and covers the eastern area of Inner Mongolia Autonomous Region and the western area of Liaoning Province. Besides, Aohan Banner has also built China Millet Museum, Dryland Farming Theme Park and the World Research and Development Base of millet varieties. The agricultural heritage theme restaurant and the farmyard providing the cooked millet are opened, and the tourism products related to the millet are also developed. Aohan Banner has become a health and wellness tourism place known beyond the Great Wall.

At the agricultural heritage theme restaurant, the agricultural symbol typical in Aohan - traditional production tools can be seen at the entrance. Such tools as the stone roller, the plough and the dustpan tell people the process of a grain of millet from the field to the dining table. The restaurant sells delicacies of Aohan millet, including ribs with millet, the millet crisp crust, etc. The food provided by the restaurant is warmly welcomed by tourists, and some diners come to Aohan to taste the delicacies there from other places designedly.

Guo Xiuling, the founder of this theme restaurant, is the archetypal character of Guo Ling in the microfilm titled *Home of Millet*. In order to conserve the agricultural heritage system and inherit the flavor of her hometown in her memory, Guo Xiuling returned to her hometown and opened this restaurant in Aohan in 2015. Based on the agricultural heritage brand, Guo Xiuling has successfully opened the first agricultural heritage theme restaurant - "Delicious Countryside Food" by means of building the ecological family farm integrated with the typical planting and the breeding, focusing on the production of the organic and ecological food, setting up a direct channel of green and organic products from fields to dining tables, developing the sightseeing agriculture and the leisure agriculture. Guo Xiuling's success has not only enlightened local farmers how to benefit from the conservation and inheritance of the agricultural heritage system, but also introduced a new way to integrate the development of the agriculture and the tourism.

小米饭农家院（敖汉旗农牧局 / 提供）
Farmyard Providing the Cooked Millet (Provided by AAHB)

Capacity Building of the Heritage Site

遗产地能力建设

CHAPTER 1 第1章

Publicity and Training Activities

宣传与培训活动

多元宣传，助力遗产保护

如今的敖汉旗有多个“金字招牌”，是全球重要农业文化遗产地，是中国重要农业文化遗产地，是“世界小米之乡”，也是世界小米大会举办地。为了在更大范围内宣传敖汉旱作农业系统，拍摄纪录片和广告、进行互联网直播、创作文学作品、制作微电影等各种形式的宣传活动都在开展，为保护与传承农业文化遗产发挥了重要作用。

《农业文化遗产的启示——旱作探源》在央视《科技苑》栏目播出。《敖汉——旱作农业探源》《秋后算账，敖汉小米过亿的秘密》和《敖汉小米八千年》专题片分别在央视《探索发现》《每日农经》和《走遍中国》栏目播出。央视《美丽中国乡村行》《从农田到餐桌》《生财有道》《大国农业》《大国根基》《粟说中国》等栏目，都对敖汉旗的农业文化遗产保护与发展进行报道。

中央电视台报道敖汉小米（敖汉宣传部 / 提供）
Aohan Millet Was Reported on China Central Television (Provided by Aohan Publicity Department)

记者在敖汉旗采访调研（敖汉旗农牧局 / 提供）
Journalists Were Interviewing and Investigating in Aohan Banner (Provided by AAHB)

《内蒙古敖汉旗保护种质资源》《敖汉小米的故事》分别荣登《人民政协报》《农民日报》等国家报刊。时长1分钟、30秒、15秒不等的广告，让“敖汉小米，熬出中国味”成为越来越多人熟悉的广告语。敖汉小米还入选“央视国家品牌计划”“一县一品”扶贫品牌。“八千粟”“兴隆沟”“孟克河”等小米品牌多次在国际农博会、农交会、中国绿博会、内蒙古绿博会、上海进博会等博览会上荣获金奖。

All Forms of Publicity Campaigns Help the Conservation of the Heritage

Nowadays, Aohan Banner has several honorable titles such as "Globally Important Agricultural Heritage Systems", "China Nationally Important Agricultural Heritage Systems", "Home of Millet in the World" and the place where the International Conference of Millet is held. In order to publicize Aohan Dryland Farming System more widely, all forms of publicity campaigns such as shooting the documentary and advertisement, live Internet broadcasts, writing literary works and making microfilms are being carried out. These publicity campaigns have played an important role in the conservation and inheritance of the agricultural heritage system.

Enlightenment of Agricultural Heritage - Origin of Dryland Farming was broadcast through the program titled *Technology Garden* on China Central Television. Feature films such as *Aohan - Origin of Dryland Farming*, *Square Accounts after the Autumn Harvest*, *Secret of Over 100 Million Outputs of Aohan Millet* and *8000-year-long History of Aohan Millet* were broadcast through the programs titled *Exploration and Discovery*, *Daily Agricultural Economy* and *Travel Around China* respectively on China Central Television. Programs such as *Travel of Beautiful China Countryside*, *From Farm to Table*, *Creating Wealth*, *Agriculture in China*, *The Power of Agriculture and Millet of China* broadcast on China Central Television have also reported the conservation and development of the agricultural heritage system of Aohan Banner.

敖汉小米入选一县一品扶贫品牌（敖汉旗农牧局 / 提供）

Aohan Millet Was Selected as the Poverty Alleviation Brand of "One County, One Speciality" (Provided by AAHB)

The article titled *Conservation of Germplasm Resources in Aohan Banner of Inner Mongolia* was published on Farmers' Daily and the article titled *Story of Aohan Millet* was published on the *Journal of the Chinese People's Political Consultative Conference*. Advertisements ranging from 1 minute, 30 seconds or 15 seconds have made the advertising slogan "Having Aohan Millet, Tasting Chinese Flavor" known by more people in China. Aohan millet has been elected into the list of National Brand Plan by China Central Television and as the poverty alleviation brand of "One County, One Speciality". Millet brands such as "Baqiansu", "Xinglonggou" and "Mengkehe" won gold awards several times at fairs such as International Agricultural Exposition, China International Agricultural Trade Fair, China Green Expo, Inner Mongolia Green Expo and China International Import Expo held in Shanghai.

参加第 13 届国际农博会（敖汉旗农牧局 / 提供）

Aohan Millet Products Were Displayed at the International Agricultural Exposition (Provided by AAHB)

敖汉小米亮相“天下粮仓 · 天猫新米节”（敖汉旗农牧局 / 提供）
Aohan Millet Was Introduced at “Ample Barn ·2018 Tmall New Rice Festival” (Provided by AAHB)

2017 年，在“天下粮仓 · 2017 天猫新米节”发布会上，敖汉旗旗长于宝君介绍了敖汉小米的历史、文化、环境、品质和发展前景等优势特点，并推荐了国家农业部食物与营养发展研究所权威发布的《敖汉小米食用指南》。在短短几分钟的推介中，天猫直播平台敖汉小米的点赞量突破 100 万。在“天下粮仓 · 2018 天猫新米节”发布会上，于宝君旗长再次以“敖汉小米四品香天下”为主题推介敖汉小米。在短时间的推介中，天猫直播平台敖汉小米的点赞量突破 300 万。

敖汉旗还将组织或参与编写的《敖汉小米香天下》《中国名牌》《天撒珍珠八千年》《中国重要农业文化遗产系列读本——内蒙古敖汉旱作农业系统》等科普读物，作为礼品赠送给前来敖汉的专家学者、投资商和洽谈伙伴们，让更多的人成为敖汉旱作农业系统的播音员、宣传员。

《敖汉旱作农业系统简明读本》
Concise Editions of Aohan Dryland Farming System

《敖汉小米甲天下》
Aohan Millet Is the Best in the World

（敖汉旗农牧局 / 提供）(Provided by AAHB)

不仅如此，敖汉旗还组织开展创作诗词歌赋、小说、散文等多种文学作品活动，为敖汉小米赋予了新的文化元素，提高了敖汉小米的知名度。著名作曲家卞留念为敖汉小米创作了主题歌曲《敖汉小米香天下》，在网络媒体广为传播，助推了敖汉小米的知名度不断提升。

In 2017, at "Ample Barn·2017 Tmall New Rice Festival"launch event, Yu Baojun, the leader of Aohan Banner, introduced the advantages of Aohan millet such as the historic culture, the environmental quality and the development prospect, and recommended the *Eating Guide of Aohan Millet* issued by the Institute of Food and Nutrition Development, Ministry of Agriculture and Rural Affairs. Within just a few minutes' introduction, more than 1,000,000 "likes" of Aohan millet were acquired on Tmall live platform. At "Ample Barn·2018 Tmall New Rice Festival"launch event, Yu Baojun, the leader of Aohan Banner, introduced Aohan millet with a slogan that "the fragrant Aohan millet is known all over the country". Within a short time of introduction, more than 3,000,000 "likes" of Aohan millet were acquired on Tmall live platform.

Promotional materials such as *The Fragrant Aohan Millet Is Known All over the Country*, *China Top Brand, 8000-year-long History of Aohan Millet* and *Serial Books about China-NIAHS - Inner Mongolia Aohan Dryland Farming System* organized or written by Aohan Banner have been sent to experts and scholars, investors and negotiation partners visiting Aohan as gifts in order to let more people publicize Aohan Dryland Farming System.

Besides, Aohan Banner has also organized to create various literary works such as poems, songs, novels and proses, to endow Aohan millet with new cultural elements, which has improved the reputation of Aohan millet. Bian Liulian, a famous composer, has written the theme song for Aohan millet titled *The Fragrant Aohan Millet Is Known All over the Country*. The song is very popular on the Internet, which has helped improve the reputation of Aohan millet.

敖汉小米宣传作品（敖汉旗农牧局 / 提供）
Promotional Works of Aohan Millet (Provided by AAHB)

《中国重要农业文化遗产系列读本——内蒙古敖汉旱作农业系统》（焦雯珺 / 摄）
Serial Books about China-NIAHS - Inner Mongolia Aohan Dryland Farming System (Taken by Jiao Wenjun)

《内蒙古敖汉旱作农业系统》是中国科学院地理科学与资源研究所自然与文化遗产研究中心策划、农业农村部支持的《中国重要农业文化遗产系列读本》之一，由中国农业出版社出版，获得赤峰市第四届社会科学优秀成果政府奖二等奖。《敖汉旱作农业系统保护与发展的思考》发表于《中国农学通报》，获得内蒙古自治区第六届社会科学优秀成果政府三等奖、赤峰市第三届社会科学优秀成果政府奖，被赤峰市图书馆永久收藏。

加强基层技术培训，助推地方发展

对外多元宣传，对内则加强培训。农业文化遗产的保护和发展离不开专业化的人才，对从事农业生产的基层一线人员的持续投入更为重要。为此，敖汉旗实施了“1+2+3”创新人才孵化计划。采用集中讲座、基地观摩、经验交流、现场辅导、外部参观、产品介绍的“六位一体”模式，与高等院校、科研院所加强产学研合作，计划利用三年时间，培育一批具有致富示范引领作用的农牧民专业合作社理事长、家庭农场主、中小微企业主、青年创业人才、返乡创业人才和经纪人“六类能人”。通过这些观念新、善经营、懂管理、带动强的新型职业农民的积极参与和奉献，传承 8 000 年历史的农业文化遗产，保障敖汉旱作农业系统的永续发展和利用。

2019 年脱贫致富带头人培训班（敖汉旗农牧局 / 提供）
Training Class for Poverty Alleviation Leaders in 2019 (Provided by AAHB)

Serial Books about China-NIAHS - Inner Mongolia Aohan Dryland Farming System, published by China Agricultural Press, won the second prize of The 4th Government Award for Outstanding Achievements on Social Science of Chifeng City. *Reflection on the Conservation and Development of Aohan Dryland Farming System*, published on Chinese Agricultural Science Bulletin, won the third prize of The 6th Government Award for Outstanding Achievements on Social Science of Inner Mongolia Autonomous Region and The 3rd Government Award for Outstanding Achievements on Social Science of Chifeng City. And it has been collected by Chifeng Library permanently.

Strengthen Technical Training at Grassroots Level and Promote the Local Development

Aohan Banner adheres to the promotion of Aohan millet in all forms outside the banner and the improvement of the training inside the banner. As the conservation and development of the agricultural heritage system needs the professional talents, it is more important to train the front-line personnel who engage in the agricultural production at grassroots level. Therefore, Aohan Banner has adopted the incubation program of "1 + 2 + 3" for the innovative talents. Aohan Banner has strengthened the industry-university-research cooperation with universities and scientific research institutions by means of "six" models such as intensive lectures, the base observation, the experience exchange, the on-site guidance, the external visit and the product introduction. Aohan Banner plans to cultivate a batch of "six kinds of capable persons" within three years, such as the direct-general of specialized cooperative composed of farmers and herdsmen, the family farmer, the medium-sized, small and micro-sized enterprise owners, the young entrepreneurial talents, the entrepreneurial talents returning to hometown from cities and the broker who are expected to lead local people to shake off poverty and become rich. Aohan Banner hopes to inherit the agricultural heritage system with an 8000-year-long history and ensure the sustainable utilization of Aohan Dryland Farming System through the way that these new kinds of skilled farmers, who have new concepts and strong leadership, and are good at operating and managing, can participate in it and make contribution to it actively.

农民现场培训（敖汉旗农牧局 / 提供）
On-site Training for Farmers (Provided by AAHB)

CHAPTER 2 第2章

S&T Cooperation and Market Development

科技合作与市场开拓

加强科技合作，促进遗产保护

由于在农业文化遗产保护与发展方面做出的卓越成就，中国科学院地理科学与资源研究所、农业部（现农业农村部）农村经济研究中心、中国农业大学人文与社会学院、中南民族大学等科研院所和高校先后将敖汉旗作为研究基地。敖汉旗也充分利用这一优势，与中国科学院地理科学与资源研究所、中国农业科学院、中国农业大学、赤峰学院、赤峰农科院等科研院所、高校建立长期战略合作协议。借助高校和科研院所雄厚的科研实力，通过开展广泛的科技合作，有效促进敖汉旗在新品种培育、旱作种植技术开发、科技人员培训、杂粮产业发展等方面的研究。

赤峰学院合作育种基地（敖汉旗农牧局 / 提供）
Cooperative Breeding Base with Chifeng College (Provided by AAHB)

专家现场指导（敖汉旗农牧局 / 提供）
On-site Guidance by Experts (Provided by AAHB)

《敖汉小米食用指南》（敖汉旗农牧局 / 提供）
Eating Guide of Aohan Millet (Provided by AAHB)

敖汉旗与农业农村部食物与营养发展研究所合作，于 2017 年 9 月出版发行了《敖汉小米食用指南》。该指南分析了敖汉小米的主要特点，发布了敖汉小米营养成分检测数据，对敖汉小米品质进行客观评价，并对敖汉小米食用方法进行推广。

为更好地开展农业文化遗产保护研究和小米产业发展研究，2017 年 9 月，由中国工程院李文华院士牵头组建的敖汉旗农业文化遗产保护与小米产业发展院士专家工作站正式成立。

《敖汉小米食用指南》发布会（敖汉旗农牧局 / 提供）
The Launch of *Eating Guide of Aohan Millet* (Provided by AAHB)

Enhance Scientific and Technological Cooperation and Promote the Conservation of the Heritage System

Thanks to the great contribution to the conservation and development of the agricultural heritage, Aohan Banner has become the research base of universities and scientific research institutions such as Institute of Geographic Sciences and Natural Resources Research, CAS, Rural Economic Research Center of the Ministry of Agriculture, College of Humanities and Social Sciences of China Agricultural University and South-central University for Nationalities. Aohan Banner has also made full use of this advantage and established long-term cooperation agreements with universities and scientific research institutions such as Chinese Academy of Sciences, China Agricultural University, Chinese Academy of Agricultural Sciences, Chifeng College and Chifeng Academy of Agricultural and Animal Husbandry Sciences. Due to the strong scientific research strength of universities and scientific research institutions, the extensive scientific and technological cooperation between Aohan Banner and them can promote Aohan Banner's research on the cultivation of new varieties, the development of the dryland farming techniques, the training of scientific and technological personnel and the development of the coarse grain industry effectively.

Aohan Banner cooperated with the Institute of Food and Nutrition Development, Ministry of Agriculture and Rural Affairs to jointly published *Eating Guide of Aohan Millet* in September 2017. The guide has analyzed the main characteristics of Aohan millet, issued the inspection data on the nutritional ingredient of Aohan millet, evaluated the quality of Aohan millet objectively and promoted the eating methods of Aohan millet.

In order to carry out the research on the conservation of the agricultural heritage and the research on the development of the millet industry better, Li Wenhua, an academician of Chinese Academy of Engineering, led to established the Academician and Expert Workstation focusing on the conservation of the agricultural heritage and the development of the millet industry officially in Aohan Banner in September 2017.

院士专家工作站牌匾（敖汉旗农牧局/提供）
The Plaque of Academician and Expert Workstation (Provided by AAHB)

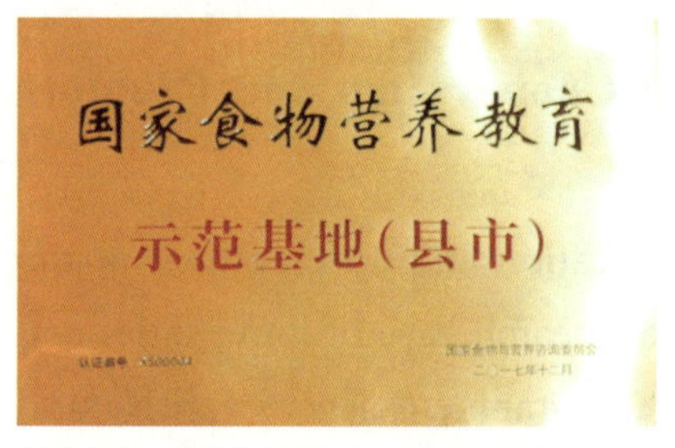

“国家食物营养教育示范基地”牌匾（敖汉旗农牧局 / 提供）
The Plaque of National Food Nutrition Education Demonstration Base (Provided by AAHB)

2017 年 12 月，敖汉旗被国家食物与营养委员会确定为首批国家食物营养教育示范基地。基地建设优质杂粮种植基地 160 万亩，其中有机杂粮基地 5 万亩，绿色杂粮基地 27.2 万亩；引进富硒谷子种植技术，种植面积 5 000 亩，通过施硒肥和喷叶肥两种形式生产富硒谷子。

在相关专家的支持和民间组织的资助下，中国科学院农业政策研究中心计划在敖汉旗建立社区种子银行，为当地居民利用传统农家品种提升自身生活质量提供新的思路，该措施不仅能增进当地居民对 8 000 年粟文化的珍视，还能推动当地农业生物多样性保护工作的开展。

扩大区域市场合作，打造农产品品牌

敖汉小米经历了从无名到有名再到知名的品牌嬗变，成为敖汉旗扩大区域市场合作、打造敖汉农产品品牌的“拳头产品”。八千粟、兴隆洼、孟克河、村头树等品牌小米远销北京、上海、广州等大城市，西北、西南、东北等地客商纷纷来敖汉建设基地，“世界小米之乡”“中国小米之乡”“国家地理标志保护产品”等招牌落地，由此带动小米市场价格由 2014 年前的每斤[①]4 元涨到 2019 年的 8~15 元。全旗每年向外输出优质谷子超过 2 亿斤，成为全国谷子市场价格信息的“晴雨表”。

区域间企业合作是市场开拓的重要途径。敖汉旗小米生产加工企业、农民专业合作社积极参加全国各地、各级别的农交会、农展会，搭建了以敖汉小米为主的杂粮农产品宣传、推介平台。敖汉旗协助承办“2017 赤峰 · 中国北方农业科技成果博览会”敖汉分会，设立了全球重要农业文化遗产——敖汉旱作农业系统展示区，取得良好的宣传效果。同时，在北京、内蒙古对口帮扶下，敖汉小米成功进入北京市海淀区政府食堂、超市发超市，也与全国各地知名企业和超市实现了农超对接。

“京蒙扶贫协作”启动仪式（敖汉旗农牧局 / 提供）
Opening Ceremony of “Beijing-Inner Mongolia Cooperation on Poverty Alleviation” (Provided by AAHB)

敖汉小米进北京超市（敖汉旗农牧局 / 提供）
Aohan Millet Is Sold at Supermarkets in Beijing (Provided by AAHB)

① 斤为旧制，1 斤为0.5千克，全书同。

In December 2017, Aohan Banner was elected as the first batch of National Food Nutrition Education Demonstration Base by National Food and Nutrition Commission. Aohan Banner has established 1,600,000 mu of quality coarse grain planting base, including 50,000 mu of organic coarse grain base and 272,000 mu of green coarse grain base. Aohan Banner has introduced the planting technique of Se-rich millet and planted 5000 mu of Se-rich millet for which the selenium fertilizer is applied and the foliar fertilizer is sprayed.

With the support of relevant experts and the economic support of non-governmental organizations, Center for Chinese Agricultural Policy of CAS plans to establish a community seed bank in Aohan Banner to provide a new way for local residents to improve their own living quality through the traditional agricultural varieties. It can not only make local residents cherish the 8000-year-long millet cultural, but also promote the conservation of local agricultural biodiversity.

Expand Regional Market Cooperation and Build Agricultural Product Brand

Aohan millet has experienced great changes from an unknown brand to a little famous one and then to a well-known one. It has now become the “key product” of Aohan Banner to expand regional cooperation and build agricultural product brands. Millet with brands such as Baqiansu, Xinglongwa, Mengkehe and Cuntoushu has been sold to large cities such as Beijing, Shanghai and Guangzhou. Investors from Xinjiang, Chengdu and Shenyang came to build their bases in Aohan Banner. As Aohan Banner acquired the titles such as “Home of Millet in the World”, “Home of Millet in China” and “National Protection Product with Geographical Indication”, the price of the millet has risen from RMB 4 yuan per jin before 2014 to RMB 8-15 yuan per jin in 2019. Due to the annual output of more than 200,000,000 jin of quality millet, Aohan Banner has become the “barometer” of the price information on the national millet market.

The interregional enterprise cooperation is an important way to expand the market. The millet production and processing enterprises, and farmers’ specialized cooperatives in Aohan Banner have actively participated in China International Agricultural Trade Fair and the agricultural product exhibitions at all levels held all over the country, and set up a promotion platform for the coarse grain products based on Aohan millet. Aohan Banner assisted to hold a branch of “2017 Chifeng.Agricultural Science and Technology Achievements Fair in Northern China” in Aohan, and set up a display area on GIAHS - Aohan Dryland Farming System, through which Aohan millet was effectively promoted. At the same time, with the counterpart assistance between Beijing and Inner Mongolia, Aohan millet has been successfully sold to the dining room of Haidian District Government of Beijing and CSF Market. Besides, Aohan Banner has also realized the farming-supermarket docking with well-known enterprises and supermarkets all over the country.

敖汉旗农村淘宝运营中心（敖汉旗农牧局 / 提供）
Cun. Taobao. Com Operation Center in Aohan Banner (Provided by AAHB)

敖汉小米进京（敖汉旗农牧局 / 提供）
Aohan Millet Is Sold in Beijing (Provided by AAHB)

为将杂粮品牌更好地推向国内和国际市场，敖汉旗还积极拓展线上销售渠道。敖汉绿色原生态杂粮已入驻淘宝网、天猫商城、京东商城、1 号店等大型网络超市。销售网络已覆盖了全国所有的二三线以上城市，相关农产品受到了北京、沈阳、广州、深圳、大连等大中城市消费者的青睐。

敖汉小米产业的蓬勃发展带来重大商机，加拿大、福建、新疆维吾尔自治区（全书简称新疆）、四川、北京等国内外客商纷纷到敖汉旗投资兴业、建设基地。山东东阿阿胶集团与敖汉旗签订了驴产业发展合作协议，建立了“战略伙伴”关系，敖汉旗成为“东阿阿胶”“双百计划”（两个“百万头”养驴基地建设计划）的实施地之一。

In order to promote its coarse grain brands to the domestic and international markets better, Aohan Banner has also expanded online sales channels actively. Green and original coarse grains of Aohan have been sold on large online supermarkets such as Taobao, Tmall, JD.com and YHD.com. The sales network of the coarse grain products of Aohan Banner has covered all second-or third-tier or above cities in the country, and the relevant agricultural products are very popular among consumers in large and medium-sized cities such as Beijing, Shenyang, Guangzhou, Shenzhen and Dalian.

The rapid development of Aohan millet industry has brought about important business opportunities. Domestic and international investors from Canada, Fujian, Xinjiang, Sichuan and Beijing came to Aohan Banner to invest in enterprises or build bases. For example, Shandong Dong'e Ejiao Group and Aohan Banner have signed a cooperation agreement with regard to the development of the donkey industry, and established a “strategic partner” relationship. Aohan Banner has become one of the implementation areas of Dong'e Ejiao Group's “Double Million Plan” (the construction plan of two “a million” donkeys raising bases).

CHAPTER
3
第3章

International and Regional Exchange
国际与区域交流

世界小米大会，搭建国际交流平台

全球重要农业文化遗产的认定为敖汉旗杂粮产业乃至全旗经济社会蓬勃发展提供了重要契机。其中，敖汉小米迅速驰名海内外，成为“世界小米之乡”的首个品牌和最大品牌。

在诸多专家的建议下，敖汉旗在全球范围内成功打造了“世界小米起源与发展国际会议”（简称“世界小米大会”）这一靓丽的名片。按照“一年一度召开、逐年不同主题”的总体设计，2014 年以来已成功举办 6 届世界小米大会，为世界了解小米、了解敖汉、了解敖汉旱作农业系统提供了重要平台。

历届世界小米大会的情况

2014 年 9 月 3 日，第一届世界小米起源与发展国际会议以谷子起源为主题，确定了敖汉旗“世界小米之乡”的地位。

2015 年 9 月 17 日，第二届世界小米起源与发展国际会议以发展为主题，产业发展、遗产传承、文化发掘成为此次会议的三大重要支撑。

2016 年 9 月 20 日，第三届世界小米起源与发展国际会议以产业为主题，进一步深入研究及展示敖汉史前文化，挖掘敖汉 8 000 年农耕的历史底蕴，开发敖汉旱作农业系统的当代价值，引领小米产业健康发展。

2017 年 9 月 21 日，第四届世界小米起源与发展国际会议以品牌与贸易为主题，推动了敖汉小米区域品牌的形成。

2018 年 9 月 8 日，第五届世界小米起源与发展国际会议以全球 / 中国重要农业文化遗产 · 敖汉旱作农业系统与乡村振兴为主题，科学谋划小米产业未来发展之路。

2019 年 9 月 1 日，第六届世界小米起源与发展国际会议以小米产业发展与乡村振兴为主题，推动小米产业初步形成。

International Conference of Millet Builds an International Communication Platform

The designation of the Globally Important Agricultural Heritage Systems has provided an important opportunity for the coarse grain industry of Aohan Banner, even the rapid social and economic development of the whole banner. Among them, Aohan millet is well-known all over the world and becomes the first and best brand of "Home of the Millet in the World".

With suggestions of many experts, Aohan Banner has successfully built an attractive card worldwide - "International Conference on the Source and Development of the Millet in the World" (hereinafter "International Conference of Millet"). In accordance with the overall design that "the conference should be held annually with different topics", 6 international conferences of millet have been held successfully since 2014, which have provided an important platform for the people all over the world to learn about the millet, Aohan and Aohan Dryland Farming System.

Information on International Conferences of Millet from 2014-2019

The 1st International Conference of Millet was held on September 3, 2014 with the Origin of the Millet as its topic. Aohan Banner's status as the "Home of the Millet in the World" was determined at this conference;

The 2nd International Conference of Millet was held on September 17, 2015 with Development as its topic. The industrial development, the heritage inheritance and the cultural excavation were the three hot issues of this conference;

The 3rd International Conference of Millet was held on September 20, 2016 with Industry as its topic. The conference focused on the further research and display of the prehistoric culture of Aohan, the excavation of the 8000-year-long farming history of Aohan, the contemporary value to develop Aohan Dryland Farming System and the healthy development of the millet industry;

The 4th International Conference of Millet was held on September 21, 2017 with Brand and Trade as its topic. The conference promoted the formation of the regional brand of Aohan millet;

The 5th International Conference of Millet was held on September 8, 2018 with GIAHS/China-NIAHS Aohan Dryland Farming System and Rural Revitalization as its topic. The conference planned the future development of the millet industry scientifically;

The 6th International Conference of Millet was held on September 1, 2019 with Development of the Millet Industry and Rural Revitalization as its topic. The conference promoted the preliminary establishment of the millet industry.

第一届世界小米大会（敖汉旗农牧局 / 提供）
The 1st International Conference of Millet (Provided by AAHB)

第一届世界小米大会以小米起源为主题，国内外专家对小米起源进行了热烈的研讨，得到敖汉旗是小米起源地之一的重要结论。大会一致决定，将敖汉旗作为“世界小米之乡”。在第一届世界小米大会成功举办后，敖汉小米拿到了 2015 年 5 月意大利米兰世界博览会的入场券，并以全球重要农业文化遗产的身份进行了参展。“孟克河”有机小米、“八千粟”绿色小米得到了国际认可，开启了国际化道路。敖汉旱作农业系统也通过图文并茂的形式向全世界进行了展示，让更多人了解敖汉 8 000 年的农耕文化。这也是继世界小米大会成功举办后，敖汉小米又一次登上国际大舞台。

一届又一届的世界小米大会确立了敖汉旗“世界小米之乡”的地位，也带来了可观的经济收益。为在更大范围内传播世界小米大会精神，会议组织形式也在不断创新。与以往四届大会不同，2018 年第五届世界小米大会首次采用 App 平台网络客户端直播。网络链接了敖汉信息网、敖汉同城等平台，通过朋友圈广泛推送，点击量达 2.02 万人次，实现了预期效果。

小米大会现场参观（敖汉旗农牧局 / 提供）
Site Visit during the 1st International Conference of Millet (Provided by AAHB)

The origin of the millet is the topic of the 1st International Conference of Millet. Experts at home and abroad discussed the origin of the millet enthusiastically at the conference and reached an important conclusion that Aohan Banner is one of the origin areas of the millet. Aohan Banner was unanimously regarded as the "Home of the Millet in the World" at the conference. After the 1st International Conference of Millet was held successfully, Aohan millet gained an entrance ticket of Expo Milano 2015 which was held in May 2015 in Italy, and participated in the exhibition as the Globally Important Agricultural Heritage System. Organic millet of "Mengkehe" and green millet of "Baqiansu" were accepted by people in the world and began the international development. Aohan Dryland Farming System was also been displayed and introduced vividly through pictures to people all over the world, which enabled more people to learn about the 8000-year-long farming culture of Aohan. This is a second time for Aohan millet to be introduced worldwide after the 1st International Conference of Millet was successfully held.

Successive international conferences of millet have confirmed the status of Aohan Banner as the "Home of the Millet in the World" and brought about considerable economic benefits. In order to spread the spirit of the international conference of millet more widely, the organizational form of the conference has also been innovated. Different from the former four conferences, the 5th International Conference of Millet held in 2018 was shown through live streaming on the networking client of APP platform for the first time. The click rate on the Internet linked platforms such as Aohan information website, Aohan intra-city website reached 20200 persons each time on the conference by means of the push message of WeChat Moments, which realized the expected promotion effect.

第五届世界小米大会（敖汉旗农牧局 / 提供）
The 5th International Conference of Millet (Provided by AAHB)

小米大会上签订合作协议（敖汉旗农牧局 / 提供）
Cooperation Agreement Signed at the International Conference of Millet (Provided by AAHB)

国际学员考察敖汉旱作农业系统（敖汉旗农牧局 / 提供）
International Trainees Were Visiting Aohan Dryland Farming System (Provided by AAHB)

敖汉旗积极开展国际合作，扩大敖汉旱作农业系统的影响力和知名度，将敖汉杂粮推向全球市场。2013 年，敖汉旗组团赴日本参加全球重要农业文化遗产论坛及展览，实现了敖汉旗杂粮产品在国外的首次展出，也在国际舞台上更好地展示了敖汉旗农业发展和农业文化遗产保护的成绩。

2017 年 7 月，在第四届东亚地区农业文化遗产研讨会上，敖汉旗分享了由农业文化遗产品牌助推地方经济发展的做法与经验，引起了日本、韩国遗产地代表和专家的高度关注，为下一步建立合作关系打下了良好基础。

2017 年 9 月，第四届全球重要农业文化遗产高级别培训班在敖汉结业，来自希腊、葡萄牙、意大利、几内亚、老挝等 19 个国家的学员实地参观考察了敖汉旗传统农家品种保护基地和丰收乡谷传统种植基地，并亲身体验谷子传统收获方式，对敖汉旗利用农业文化遗产做大敖汉小米品牌给予大力赞赏。

缘于敖汉小米的世界影响，2018 年 6 月小轮车国际赛场在敖汉旗落地建成。这是中国至今唯一一个达到奥运级别的小轮车竞速赛道，获得了国际自行车运动联盟的官方赛道认证。小轮车国际赛场目前已圆满承办多项国际赛事，吸引了来自比利时、荷兰、澳大利亚、新西兰、西班牙、瑞典、英国、俄罗斯等 20 多个国家、30 余支车队的职业运动员参赛。敖汉小米等一系列地方产品也借此机会得到了更广泛的宣传。

敖汉旗小轮车国际赛场举行比赛（敖汉旗农牧局 / 提供）
Competition Held at International Competition Terrain of Bicycle Motocross in Aohan Banner (Provided by AAHB)

Aohan Banner has actively carried out the international cooperation in order to increase the influence and reputation of Aohan Dryland Farming System and introduce Aohan coarse grains to the global market. In 2013, Aohan Banner organized a group to participate in the GIAHS Forum and the exhibition during the forum held in Japan, through which the coarse grain products produced in Aohan Banner were displayed overseas for the first time. The agricultural development of Aohan Banner and the achievement of the agricultural heritage conservation were also displayed on the international stage.

In July 2017, at the 4th Conference of the East Asia Research Association for Agricultural Heritage Systems, Aohan Banner shared its experience in the local economic development promoted by the agricultural heritage brand, which attracted the high attention of representatives and experts from the heritage sites in Japan and South Korea. It has laid a solid foundation for the next cooperation.

In September 2017, the 4th high-level training class on the Globally Important Agricultural Heritage Systems ended in Aohan Banner. During the training, trainees from 19 countries such as Greece, Portugal, Italy, the Republic of Guinea and Laos visited the protection base of the traditional varieties and the traditional millet planting base at Fengshou Township of Aohan Banner, and experienced the traditional harvest approach of the millet. They all praised Aohan Banner's success in making Aohan millet brand known by mean of the agricultural heritage conservation.

Thanks to the worldwide influence of Aohan millet, the international competition terrain of bicycle motocross was built in Aohan Banner in June 2018. It has been the only international competition terrain of bicycle motocross which reaches the standard of Olympic Games so far in China. And Aohan Banner acquired the official certification of its bicycle motocross terrain issued by Union Cycliste International. Many international competitions have been held at the international competition terrain of bicycle motocross, which have attracted professional athletes in more than 30 bicycle motocross fleets coming from more than 20 countries including Belgium, Netherlands, Australia, New Zealand, Spain, Sweden, UK and Russia, etc. Aohan millet and serials of local products have also been promoted during the competitions.

美国地理频道《寻脉》到敖汉旗（敖汉旗农牧局 / 提供）
The Program of *Searching for the Root* on National Geographic Channel of the United States Came to Aohan (Provided by AAHB)

2018 年 8 月，由英国、泰国、新加坡等国组成的美国地理频道《寻脉》摄制组走进敖汉旗寻至敖汉小米，通过《寻脉》这个节目向全世界展示敖汉旗农业文化遗产保护的丰硕成果。

敖汉旱作农业系统的保护与利用引起国际社会关注。联合国粮食及农业组织专家在接受中央电视台的采访时表示，“作为全球重要农业文化遗产地，敖汉用自己的智慧和巧妙的耕作方法不断提升农产品的价值和农民自身的收益，不仅有助于当地环境和生态系统的保护，也为世界农业可持续发展和应对气候变化提供了更多思路。”世界粮食计划署官员调研敖汉旱作农业系统后表示，“敖汉旱作农业系统是中国农业的一个范例，展示了一种更好的耕作方式，应该在其他地区得到推广和复制”。国际生物多样性中心专家到敖汉旗调研传统农家品种保护情况后表示，“敖汉旱作农业系统中生物多样性丰富，通过与农民座谈发现，时至今日农户家中仍留存着大量的传统农家品种，这些珍贵的种质资源在应对半干旱地区土壤、气候环境上具有不可取代性，是维持农业可持续发展、培育优质农作物新品种、解决人类未来粮食安全的重要物质保证。”

In August 2018, the camera crew of *Searching for the Root* on National Geographic Channel of the United States composed of members from UK, Thailand, Singapore and so on came to Aohan Banner to look for Aohan millet. The fruitful achievement on the conservation of the agricultural heritage system in Aohan Banner has been introduced to the world through this program.

The conservation and utilization of Aohan Dryland Farming System have aroused attention from the international society. An expert from Food and Agriculture Organization of the United Nations said when he accepted the interview of China Central Television, "As a GIAHS site, Aohan has used wisdom and skillful farming methods to improve the value of agricultural products and farmers' income continuously It is helpful not only to protect the local environment and the ecological system, but also to provide more ways of the sustainable development of the international agriculture and the battle against the climate change." An officer from World Food Programme said after he investigated the dryland farming system in Aohan Banner, "Aohan Dryland Farming System is an example of China's agriculture. It shows a better farming approach, which should be promoted and duplicated in other areas." An expert from Biodiversity International said after he investigated the conservation of the traditional crop varieties in Aohan Banner, "The biodiversity in Aohan Dryland Farming System is very immense. When I talk with local farmers, I find that they still keep many traditional crop varieties at home till now. These valuable germplasm resources are irreplaceable to cope with the soil and the climate environment in semi-arid areas and are an important material guarantee to maintain the sustainable development of the agriculture, cultivate quality and new crop varieties and solve the future food security of human beings."

世界粮食计划署调研敖汉旗（敖汉旗农牧局 / 提供）
Officials of World Food Programme Were Investigating Aohan Banner (Provided by AAHB)

CHAPTER 4

第 4 章

New Farmers in the Internet Age

互联网时代的新农人

"村头树"小米（敖汉旗农牧局 / 提供）
"Cuntoushu" Millet (Provided by AAHB)

互联网的出现和崛起，给信息的传播途径、企业的生产模式、产品的流通方式以及人们的消费行为带来了巨大的改变。农产品的线上营销成为农业文化遗产地适应互联网时代的先驱行为。互联网营销不仅将商品销往全国各地，更将农业文化遗产的影响力带到千家万户。

为了在电子商务催生商业变革的历史大潮中站稳脚跟，敖汉旗着力打造以绿色杂粮为主产品的电商基地，让本土杂粮接轨新兴市场，并率先启动了"国家电子商务进农村"示范项目。在这一过程中，敖汉旗涌现出一批创新农产品营销模式的新农人，陈鑫垚和刘海庆就是其中的典型代表。

电商引领网络销售，造福家乡共谋富裕

"村头树"是敖汉旗首批涉农网店之一，通过销售绿色杂粮不仅为自身带来了巨大收益，还在当地掀起了网络销售的风潮。"村头树"的创始人陈鑫垚毕业于北京师范大学，创业前已经是国内知名门户网站总部博客频道主编。2011 年，他在事业如日中天时毅然请辞，将目光聚焦在如朝阳初上的涉农电子商务行业。陈鑫垚和弟弟将自家土地作为生产基地，弟弟陈鑫利任生产经理，严把种植、收购、包装、发货整条生产线，而他则驻扎北京负责市场销售与推广。不到 3 年的时间，"村头树"杂粮店的年收入已从 10 万元攀升至 80 万元。

Due to the emergence and rise of Internet, great changes have taken place in the way of information dissemination, the production mode of enterprises, the circulation mode of products and people's consuming behaviors. Online marketing of the agricultural products has become a pioneering method for the agricultural heritage site to adapt to the Internet Age. Internet marketing not only sells goods nationwide, but also conveys the influence of the agricultural heritage to thousands of households.

In order to keep competitive in the business transformation induced by the e-commerce, Aohan Banner commits itself to developing the e-commerce base focusing on green coarse grains for the purpose of linking local coarse grain to the emerging market. Aohan Banner is the first to launch the "Introducing National E-commerce to Rural Areas" demonstration project. During this process, a batch of new farmers who innovate the marketing model of the agricultural products appear in Aohan Banner. Chen Xinyao and Liu Haiqing are typical representatives of them.

E-commerce Promotes Online Sales and Helps Hometown Become Rich

"Cuntoushu" is one of the first batch of online stores selling agricultural products in Aohan Banner. "Cuntoushu" has not only earned a lot by selling green coarse grains, but also raised the wave of online sales. Chen Xinyao, the founder of "Cuntoushu", graduated from Beijing Normal University. He had been a chief editor of the blog channel at Sohu headquarters before he started his business in Aohan Banner. In 2011, he resigned resolutely when his career was at a best moment. He then focused on the rising e-commerce industry related to agricultural products. He and his brother use their own land as the production base. Chen Xinli, Chen Xinyao's brother, works as the production manager of "Cuntoushu" and is responsible for the whole production line including the planting, purchase, packaging and delivery. Chen Xinyao himself stays at Beijing and is responsible for sales and promotion. In less than 3 years, the annual income of "Cuntoushu" coarse grain store has increased from RMB 100,000 yuan to RMB 800,000 yuan.

垄施农家肥（敖汉旗农牧局 / 提供）
Ridge Application of Farmyard Manure (Provided by AAHB)

“村头树”杂粮在生产上，选用营养价值高、适应当地气候条件的优质种子，种植前施用农家肥作为底肥，精耕细作；在加工上，尽量保持原生态，避免养分流失，保留最天然的形态；在包装上，优选国内知名品牌供应商以确保安全。“村头树”网店注册商标并成立了敖汉旗村头树农产品销售有限公司，建起了“村头树”合作社，发展“公司 + 合作社 + 农户”模式，统一管理，确保质量。

丰收时刻（敖汉旗农牧局 / 提供）
Harvest Moment (Provided by AAHB)

“村头树”网店在线上销售刚刚兴起时加入电商队伍，经过长足的发展，在敖汉旗杂粮电商界掌握了一定的话语权。“村头树”模式经推广后成为大家效仿的榜样，为敖汉旗网店促就业提供了动力和经验。

大学生返乡创业，打造营销新模式

刘海庆是敖汉旗兴隆洼镇嘎岔村人，大学毕业后回到家乡。2017 年年初，他利用微信朋友圈“众筹”模式开展营销，联系了 100 人，每人认购小米 10 斤，前期筹集到 1.6 万元人民币并以此为启动资金，刘海庆依托敖汉旗的生态环境优势和传统生产技术，开展绿色生态的谷子种植，收获后再统一发货。

With regard to the production, "Cuntoushu" coarse grain chooses quality seeds with high nutritional values and the adaptability to local climate conditions. Before the seeds are planted, the farmyard manure is applied as the base fertilizer. The intensive cultivation is adopted during the growing period; with regard to the processing, the most natural state of the coarse grain is kept without being polished and dyed in order to avoid the nutrient loss; with regard to its packaging, "Cuntoushu" has chosen the same manufacturer as Yili's sealing bag to produce its inner bag, and the same manufacturer as Xiaomi smartphone's packing box to produce its outer box. After the increase of its sales volume, "Cuntoushu" registered the trademark and founded Aohan Banner Cuntoushu Agricultural Products Sales Co., Ltd. and established a "Cuntoushu" cooperative. "Cuntoushu" has developed "company+ cooperative+ farmers" model and adopted uniform management to ensure the quality.

"Cuntoushu" online store joined the e-commerce industry at the beginning of online sales. After several years' development, it has now held the power of speech in the e-commerce circle of the coarse grain in Aohan Banner. After being promoted, the model of "Cuntoushu" has now become an example copied by many people, which has provided a driving force and experience for online store employment of Aohan Banner.

College Student Returns to Hometown to Start a Business and Creates a New Marketing Model

Liu Haiqing, born in Gacha Village, Xinglongwa Town, Aohan Banner, returned to hometown after graduation from the university. At the beginning of 2017, he contacted 100 people by means of "crowdfunding" in WeChat Moments, and finally raised RMB 16,000 yuan as each person offered to purchase 10 jin of millet. Liu Haiqing used the money he raised as the start-up capital, based on the ecological and environmental advantages and traditional production techniques of Aohan Banner, to plant green and ecological millet and he delivered the millet uniformly after the harvest.

刘海庆参加第六届南南论坛（敖汉旗农牧局 / 提供）
Liu Haiqing attended the 6th South South Forum (Provided by AAHB)

刘海庆在自家的土地上采用传统方法进行种植，利用敖汉旗积温高、昼夜温差大、光照充足的自然优势，仅施用少量农家肥，不施用农药、化肥、除草剂等，生产出的小米色泽清新、营养丰富。虽然种植面积只有 5 亩，但是亩产最低 200 斤，因此除满足订单外还有盈余。而每亩的基本投入不足 200 元，效益极为可观。

传统营销方式是先生产、再销售，而刘海庆反其道而行，成为顺互联网之势，创新营销模式的弄潮儿。以众筹为途径的“年初认购、计划种植、收后配送”的模式通过了市场的检验。刘海庆在尝到“众筹”的甜头后，也敏锐地乘胜追击，成立了兴隆洼小米生态种植专业合作社，带领村民开展绿色生态的谷子种植，更有养殖户加入为生产带来更多的农家肥。

刘海庆的返乡创业之路不止于此。成立合作社的第一年，刘海庆就带领社员策划了“第一届探寻世界小米发源地”大学生夏令营。外面的青年人走进村子，与村民同吃同住。他们将外面的新事物介绍给村民，而村民则把日积月累的劳动经验和小米文化分享给他们。当这些青年人走出村子时，也将旱作农耕文化带走，从而让更多的人了解敖汉旱作农业系统。

大学生夏令营活动（敖汉旗农牧局 / 提供）
The Summer Camp for College Students (Provided by AAHB)

Liu Haiqing adopted traditional methods to plant millet on his family's land. Thanks to the natural advantages of Aohan Banner such as high accumulated temperature, large difference in temperature between day and night, and abundant sunlight, only a little farmyard manure was applied on his farmland without using the pesticide, the chemical fertilizer and the herbicide. The millet planted by Liu Haiqing had natural color and rich nutrition. Although the planting area was only 5 mu, the minimum yield was 200 jin per mu. Therefore, he still had some millet left after delivering the millet ordered previously. In consideration of less than RMB 200 yuan per mu of the basic input, his benefits were considerable.

村民与大学生交流（敖汉旗农牧局 / 提供）
Villagers Were Communicating with College Students (Provided by AAHB)

The traditional marketing method is the production first with sales following it. However, Liu Haiqing did oppositely. He became the first one to innovate the marketing model and follow the trend of Internet. His model of "subscription at the beginning of the year, planting under the plan and delivery after the harvest" made through the crowdfunding has been proved successful in the market. After gaining the benefits of "crowdfunding", Liu Haiqing sharply caught the opportunity and established Xinglongwa Millet Ecological Planting Specialized Cooperative to lead farmers to plant green and ecological millet. As of the end of 2019, the millet planting base with an area of 300 mu has been established, and its farmyard manure has increased as more farmers joined the cooperative.

Liu Haiqing has done more than that after he returned to his hometown from cities. During the first year when he set up the cooperative, Liu Haiqing led cooperative members to plan a summer camp for college students themed "The 1st Exploration of the Origin of the Millet in the World". When young people entered into the village, they lived and ate together with villagers. They introduced new things outside to villagers, while villagers shared their labor experiences accumulated for many years and the culture related to the millet with them. When these young people walked out of the village, they introduced the dryland farming culture to more people, which enabled more people to learn about Aohan Dryland Farming System.

为了动员更多的村民参与进来，2018 年夏天，刘海庆带领合作社策划了“第一届敖汉小米音乐会暨敖汉旱作故事全球重要农业文化遗产分享会”。依托农业文化遗产地优势，通过众筹办会的方式，让来自全国各地的朋友参与其中。小米音乐会不仅吸引更多村民加入合作社，也向外界的世界传递出合作社和敖汉小米的声音。

在互联网时代，信息呈网络化传播，借助新型营销模式，可以让农产品的销售额呈几何型增长，也让遗产地的影响力呈裂变式增加。敖汉旗的实践经验表明，农业文化遗产和互联网营销可以有机结合，形成新的“生产—加工—销售”链条，从而实现农业文化遗产的动态保护和可持续发展。

刘海庆在音乐会上（敖汉旗农牧局 / 提供）
Liu Haiqing Made a Speech at the Millet Concert (Provided by AAHB)

In order to mobilize more villagers to participate in the cooperative, Liu Haiqing led the cooperative members to plan “The 1st Aohan Millet Concert and The Sharing Session on Aohan Dryland Farming Story about GIAHS”. The activity involves friends from all over the country to participate in it through the crowdfunding based on the advantages of agricultural heritage site. The millet concert has not only attracted more farmers to participate in the cooperative, but also introduced the cooperative and Aohan millet to more people in the country.

In the Internet Age, the information spreads via the Internet very rapidly. The new marketing model can not only increase the sales volume of agricultural products geometrically, but also make the influence of the heritage site increase explosively. The practical experience of Aohan Banner proves that the agricultural heritage can be closely combined with the Internet marketing, which can form the new chain of “production-processing-sales” in an effort to realize the dynamic conservation and sustainable development of the agricultural heritage.

CHAPTER 5 第5章

Heritage Conservation Promotes Poverty Alleviation

遗产保护助推脱贫攻坚

产业扶贫

全球重要农业文化遗产的认定为敖汉旗小米产业发展提供了重要契机。敖汉旗在搜集传统谷子品种的基础上，选择口感好、味道香、受市场欢迎的金苗和红谷两个传统品种进行推广。积极打造敖汉小米区域公用品牌，使敖汉小米从无名到有名再到知名，成为敖汉旗扩大区域市场合作、打造敖汉农产品品牌的“拳头产品”。截至 2019 年，敖汉旗共建设优质谷子生产基地 92 万亩，其中绿色生产基地 27 万亩，有机生产基地 5 万亩；培育龙头企业 34 家，合作社 366 家；采用“龙头企业 + 合作社 + 基地 + 农户”的模式，引领全旗 56 118 户农户发展小米产业，带动 7 913 户贫困户增收脱贫。

优质谷子生产基地（敖汉旗农牧局 / 提供）
Quality Millet Production Base (Provided by AAHB)

随着敖汉小米品牌影响力逐年增强，敖汉旗谷子种植面积逐年扩大，“种谷养驴”成为当地的扶贫产业之一。2015 年，敖汉旗引进山东东阿阿胶集团，建设 6 000 头黑毛驴的养殖基地。敖汉旗成为“东阿阿胶”“双百计划”的实施地之一。敖汉旗出台了《敖汉旗扶持肉驴产业发展实施方案》，与东阿阿胶集团共建养驴扶贫担保基金，通过贷款资金对毛驴养殖户进行扶持。每户可购买 6~8 头基础母驴，以母驴年均产 0.65 个驹驴计算，每户可年出栏 4~5 头毛驴。截至 2019 年年底，总共购进基础母驴 8 005 头，项目覆盖 5 337 户 11 207 人。

Poverty Alleviation through Industrial Development

The GIAHS designation has provided an important opportunity for the industrial development of Aohan millet. Aohan Banner, based on the collection of traditional varieties, chooses two traditional varieties named Jinmiao and Honggu to promote, which taste good, smell fragrant, and are very popular in the market. Aohan Banner has actively built the regional public brand of Aohan millet, which helps the development of Aohan millet from an unknown brand to a little famous one and then to a well-known one. Aohan millet has now become the "key product" of Aohan Banner to expand regional cooperation and build agricultural product brands. As of 2019, Aohan Banner has totally built 61,333 ha of quality millet production base, of which 18,000 ha is the green production base and 3,333 ha is the organic production base; Aohan Banner has cultivated 34 leading enterprises and 366 cooperatives; Aohan Banner adopts "leading enterprises + cooperatives + bases + farmers" model to guide 56,118 households to develop the millet industry and helps 7,913 poverty-stricken households to increase incomes and shake off poverty.

As the influence of Aohan millet brand increases, the planting area of millet in Aohan Banner is increasing each year. "Planting millet and raising donkeys" has become one of local poverty alleviation industries. In 2015, Aohan Banner attracted Shandong Dong'e Ejiao Group to build a breeding base raising 6,000 black donkeys. Aohan Banner has become one of the implementation areas of Dong'e Ejiao Group's "Double Million Plan" (the construction plan of two "a million" donkeys raising bases). Aohan Banner issued *Implementation Plan on Supporting the Development of Meat Donkey Industry in Aohan Banner* and established a guarantee fund for poverty alleviation through raising donkeys jointly with Dong'e Ejiao Group. Aohan Banner provided support for households raising donkeys through the loans. Each household can buy 6 to 8 basic mares. Each household can sell 4 to 5 donkeys annually if a mare can produce 0.65 foal on average each year. As of the end of 2019, Aohan Banner has totally purchased 8,005 basic mares and the project covers 5,337 households of 11,207 people.

黑毛驴养殖基地（敖汉旗农牧局 / 提供）
The Breeding Base of Black Donkeys (Provided by AAHB)

电商扶贫

敖汉旗积极将电商产业发展与扶贫产品有机结合，助力脱贫攻坚。2016 年，敖汉旗与阿里巴巴签订战略合作协议，“敖汉小米”进入阿里巴巴“淘香甜”销售渠道，“敖汉小米官方旗舰店”在天猫网正式上线运营。2017—2018 年，敖汉旗主要领导连续两次参加在阿里巴巴总部召开的新米节发布会，亲自为“敖汉小米”代言，助推敖汉小米走进千家万户。2018 年 1 月，阿里巴巴与敖汉旗共同举办了“寻味中国 · 年味厨房——走进敖汉旗”网络直播节目，通过湖南卫视、淘宝直播、优酷直播等节目宣传“敖汉小米”。

一系列促销宣传活动，收到了良好效果。2018 年，敖汉小米网上销售收入超过 1 200 万元，敖汉旗入选阿里巴巴全国十大“电商脱贫样板县”，被命名为全国农业核心产区标准化生产基地、兴农扶贫县域官方服务站。阿里巴巴确定在敖汉小米核心产区帮扶 500 户贫困户脱贫，提供敖汉小米全产业链扶持。2019 年阿里巴巴与刘僧、惠隆、禾为贵三家企业签订了 4 000 亩“淘香甜”小米基地合同。三家企业与贫困户签约，以每亩地每年 500 元的价格一次性给付贫困户三年租金。有劳动能力的贫困户还可以到小米基地打工，进一步增加收入。

旱作农业景观（敖汉旗农牧局 / 提供）
Dryland Farming Landscape (Provided by AAHB)

Poverty Alleviation through E-commerce

Aohan Banner has actively combined the development of the e-commerce industry and the poverty alleviation products to help farmers shake off poverty. In 2016, Aohan Banner signed a strategic cooperation agreement with Alibaba Group, through which "Aohan Millet" entered "Taoxiangtian" sales channel of Alibaba and "Aohan Millet Official Flagship Store" was officially operated on Tmall.com. From 2017 to 2018, main leaders of Aohan Banner participated in the launch events for the new rice festival at the headquarters of Alibaba for twice and spoke for "Aohan Millet" personally, which helped Aohan millet enter thousands of households. In January 2018, Alibaba and Aohan Banner jointly held a live program via Internet titled "Taste of China.Kitchen at Spring Festival - Entering Aohan Banner", which was broadcast through Hunan Satellite TV, Taobaolive.com, live.youku.com, etc. to publicize "Aohan Millet".

A serial of promotion and publicity activities have acquired good effects. In 2018, the online sales amount of Aohan millet was more than RMB 12,000,000 yuan. Aohan Banner was elected as one of top 10 "Poverty Alleviation Model County via E-commerce" by Alibaba, and was given the name of the standard production base of national agricultural core production area and the official service station at county level of poverty alleviation. Alibaba has determined to help 500 households to shake off poverty in the core production area of Aohan millet and provide the whole industrial chain support of Aohan millet. In 2019, Alibaba signed a 4000-mu "Taoxiangtian" millet base contract with three companies such as Liu Seng, Huilong and Heweigui. The three companies then signed with farmers and paid three-year rents to poverty-stricken farmers in a lump sum as per the price of RMB 500 yuan per year per mu. Previously the rent of RMB 100 yuan per year per mu is not wanted by anyone, but now farmers can acquire RMB 400 yuan increase per year per mu. The poverty-stricken farmers who are able to work can work at the millet base to increase their incomes further.

丰收（敖汉旗农牧局/提供）
A Bumper Harvest (Provided by AAHB)

收获（敖汉旗农牧局 / 提供）
Harvest (Provided by AAHB)

截至 2019 年年底，敖汉旗电子商务全年交易额 13.2 亿元，同比增长 33%，全年网络零售额达 8 500 万元。全旗现有电商企业、网店、知名微商 4 000 多家，从业、就业人员 7 000 多人，直接、间接拉动就业 3.2 万人，206 个服务站辐射带动 26 409 户贫困户通过电子商务实现增收节支。

广告扶贫

2019 年 4 月 1 日，敖汉小米作为中央广播电视总台“广告精准扶贫”项目的入选产品，开始在 CCTV-1、CCTV-2、CCTV-3、CCTV-4 等 15 个频道免费播出广告，每天播出频率高达 20 次。在广告投放期间，敖汉小米的整体销量较上年同期增长了 3 倍，其中官方旗舰店的增长最为显著，单个店铺销量比上年同期增长了近十倍，其他小米企业店铺也都增长了 3~5 倍。小米扶贫广告的播出，促进了当地以小米为主的农产品的销售，也吸引了国内一些大企业、大超市纷纷到敖汉投资、采购。

小米扶贫广告的播出还获得了巨大的社会效益。一句“敖汉小米，熬出中国味”，瞬间让全国人民知道了敖汉旗。作为全球重要农业文化遗产的敖汉旱作农业系统以及旱作农业出产的其他农产品，也因此显著提高了知名度。

As of the end of 2019, the total transaction volume of e-commerce in Aohan Banner has reached RMB 1,320,000,000 yuan throughout the whole year, increasing by 33% year on year, and the retail sales via Internet has reached RMB 85,000,000 yuan throughout the whole year. There are more than 4000 e-commerce enterprises, online stores and famous WeChat businesses totally, employing more than 7000 owners and employees. 32000 persons are directly or indirectly helped for their employment. 206 service centers have helped 26,409 poverty-stricken households to increase incomes while cutting down expenses by means of e-commerce.

Poverty Alleviation through Advertisement

As Aohan millet was selected as the product of "targeted poverty alleviation through advertisement" project initiated by China Media Group, the advertisement of Aohan millet began to be broadcast on 15 channels on April 1, 2019 including CCTV-1, CCTV-2, CCTV-3 and CCTV-4 free of charge for 20 times each day. During the advertisement, the total sales amount of Aohan millet has tripled compared to the same period of last year. The sales of the official flagship store are the largest, having increased nearly ten times compared to the same period of the previous year, and the sales of other millet enterprises' stores have also increased three to five times. The broadcast of the poverty alleviation advertisement on the millet has promoted the sales of agricultural products especially the millet, and attracted some large domestic enterprises and supermarkets came to Aohan for purchase and investment.

广告精准扶贫（敖汉旗农牧局 / 提供）
Targeted Poverty Alleviation Through Advertisement (Provided by AAHB)

The broadcast of the poverty alleviation advertisement on the millet has brought about huge social benefits. The slogan "Having Aohan Millet, Tasting Chinese Flavor" has made Aohan Banner known by people all over the country immediately. As a result, the reputation of Aohan Dryland Farming System as a GIAHS, and other agricultural products produced through the dryland agriculture have also increased significantly.

扶贫广告（敖汉旗农牧局 / 提供）
Poverty Alleviation Advertisement (Provided by AAHB)

Appendix
附录

全球重要农业文化遗产名录

2002年，联合国粮食及农业组织（FAO）发起了全球重要农业文化遗产（Globally Important Agricultural Heritage Systems，GIAHS）保护项目，旨在建立全球重要农业文化遗产及其有关的景观、生物多样性、知识和文化保护体系，并在世界范围内得到认可与保护，使之成为可持续管理的基础。根据FAO的定义，GIAHS是"农村与其所处环境长期协同进化和动态适应下所形成的独特的土地利用系统和农业景观，这些系统与景观具有丰富的生物多样性，而且可以支撑当地社会经济与文化发展的需要，有利于促进区域可持续发展"。截至2020年4月，全球共有22个国家的59个传统农业系统被认定为全球重要农业文化遗产；中国有15项全球重要农业文化遗产，位居全球之首。

The List of Globally Important Agricultural Heritage Systems

In 2002, Food and Agriculture Organization of the United Nations (FAO) launched an initiative on the conservation of the Globally Important Agricultural Heritage Systems (GIAHS). It aims to establish a conservation system of the globally important agricultural heritage systems and their landscape, biodiversity, knowledge and culture, make them accepted and protected worldwide and make them become the foundation of the sustainable management. GIAHS are defined by FAO as "remarkable land use systems and landscapes which are rich in biological diversity evolving from the co-adaptation of a rural community/population with its environment and its needs and aspirations for sustainable development". As of April 2020, there are 59 traditional agricultural systems from 22 countries designated as GIAHS by FAO; China has 15 designations which outnumber other countries.

全球重要农业文化遗产（59 项）

序号	区域	国家	系统名称	FAO 批准年份
1	亚洲 Asia（9 国，40 项）	中国 China（15 项）	中国浙江青田稻鱼共生系统 Qingtian Rice-fish Culture System, China	2005
2			中国江西万年稻作文化系统 Wannian Traditional Rice Culture System, China	2010
3			中国云南红河哈尼稻作梯田系统 Honghe Hani Rice Terraces System, China	2010
4			中国贵州从江侗乡稻—鱼—鸭系统 Congjiang Dong's Rice-fish-duck System, China	2011
5			中国云南普洱古茶园与茶文化系统 Pu'er Traditional Tea Agrosystem, China	2012
6			中国内蒙古敖汉旱作农业系统 Aohan Dryland Farming System, China	2012
7			中国浙江绍兴会稽山古香榧群 Shaoxing Kuaijishan Ancient Chinese Torreya, China	2013
8			中国河北宣化城市传统葡萄园 Urban Agricultural Heritage of Xuanhua Grape Gardens, China	2013
9			中国陕西佳县古枣园 Jiaxian Traditional Chinese Date Gardens, China	2014
10			中国江苏兴化垛田传统农业系统 Xinghua Duotian Agrosystem, China	2014
11			中国福建福州茉莉花与茶文化系统 Fuzhou Jasmine and Tea Culture System, China	2014
12			中国甘肃迭部扎尕那农林牧复合系统 Diebu Zhagana Agriculture-forestry-animal husbandry Composite System,China	2017
13			中国浙江湖州桑基鱼塘系统 Zhejiang Huzhou Mulberry-dyke and Fish-pond System, China	2017
14			中国南方山地稻作梯田系统 Rice Terraces System in Southern Mountainous and Hilly Areas, China	2018
15			中国山东夏津黄河故道古桑树群 Traditional Mulberry System in Xiajin's Ancient Yellow River Course, China	2018
16		菲律宾 Philippines（1 项）	菲律宾伊富高稻作梯田系统 Ifugao Rice Terraces, Philippines	2005
17		印度 India（3 项）	印度克什米尔藏红花农业系统 Saffron Heritage of Kashmir, India	2011

（续表）

序号	区 域	国 家	系统名称	FAO 批准年份
18	亚洲 Asia（9 国，40 项）	印度 India （3 项）	印度科拉普特传统农业系统 Koraput Traditional Agriculture Systems, India	2012
19			印度喀拉拉邦库塔纳德海平面下农耕文化系统 Kuttanad Below Sea Level Farming System, India	2013
20		日本 Japan （11 项）	日本金泽能登半岛山地与沿海乡村景观 Noto's Satoyama and Satoumi, Japan	2011
21			日本新潟佐渡岛稻田—朱鹮共生系统 Sado's Satoyama in Harmony with Japanese Crested Ibis, Japan	2011
22			日本熊本阿苏可持续草原农业系统 Managing Aso Grasslands for Sustainable Agriculture, Japan	2013
23			日本静冈传统茶—草复合系统 Traditional Tea-grass Integrated System in Shizuoka, Japan	2013
24			日本大分国东半岛林—农—渔复合系统 Kunisaki Peninsula Usa Integrated Forestry, Agriculture and Fisheries System, Japan	2013
25			日本岐阜长良川香鱼养殖系统 The Ayu of Nagara River System, Japan	2015
26			日本和歌山南部—田边梅子生产系统 Minabe-Tanabe Ume System, Japan	2015
27			日本宫崎高千穗—椎叶山山地农林复合系统 Takachihogo-shiibayama Mountainous Agriculture and Forestry System, Japan	2015
28			日本宫城尾崎基于传统水资源管理的可持续农业系统 Osaki Kodo's Sustainable Agriculture System Based on Traditional Water Management, Japan	2017
29			日本德岛 Nishi-Awa 地域山地陡坡农作系统 Nishi-Awa Steep Slope Land Agriculture System, Japan	2018
30			日本静冈传统山葵种植系统 Traditional Wasabi Cultivation in Shizuoka, Japan	2018
31		韩国 Korea （4 项）	韩国青山岛板石梯田农作系统 Traditional Gudeuljang Irrigated Rice Terraces in Cheongsando, Korea	2014
32			韩国济州岛石墙农业系统 Jeju Batdam Agricultural System, Korea	2014
33			韩国花开传统河东茶农业系统 Traditional Hadong Tea Agrosystem in Hwagae-myeon, Korea	2017
34			韩国锦山传统人参种植系统 Geumsan Traditional Ginseng Agricultural System, Korea	2018

（续表）

序号	区 域	国 家	系统名称	FAO 批准年份
35	亚洲 Asia（9 国，40 项）	斯里兰卡 Sri Lanka（1 项）	斯里兰卡干旱地区梯级池塘—村庄系统 The Cascaded Tank-village Systems in the Dry Zone of Sri Lanka	2017
36		孟加拉国 Bangladesh（1 项）	孟加拉国浮田农作系统 Floating Garden Agricultural System, Bangladesh	2015
37		阿联酋 UAE（1 项）	阿联酋艾尔—里瓦绿洲传统椰枣种植系统 Al Ain and Liwa Historical Date Palm Oases, the United Arab Emirates	2015
38		伊朗 Iran（3 项）	伊朗喀山坎儿井灌溉系统 Qanat Irrigated Agricultural Heritage Systems of Kashan, Iran	2014
39			伊朗乔赞葡萄生产系统 Grape Production System and Grape-based Products, Iran	2018
40			伊朗戈纳巴德基于坎儿井灌溉藏红花种植系统 Qanat-based Saffron Farming System in Gonabad, Iran	2018
41	非洲 Africa（6 国，8 项）	阿尔及利亚 Algeria（1 项）	阿尔及利亚埃尔韦德绿洲农业系统 Ghout System, Algeria	2005
42		突尼斯 Tunisia（1 项）	突尼斯加法萨绿洲农业系统 Gafsa Oases, Tunisia	2005
43		肯尼亚 Kenya（1 项）	肯尼亚马赛草原游牧系统 Oldonyonokie/Olkeri Maasai Pastoralist Heritage, Kenya	2008
44		坦桑尼亚 Tanzania（2 项）	坦桑尼亚马赛草原游牧系统 Engaresero Maasai Pastoralist Heritage Area, Tanzania	2008
45			坦桑尼亚基哈巴农林复合系统 Shimbwe Juu Kihamba Agro-forestry Heritage Site, Tanzania	2008
46		摩洛哥 Morocco（2 项）	摩洛哥阿特拉斯山脉绿洲农业系统 Oases System in Atlas Mountainous, Morocco	2011
47			摩洛哥索阿卜—曼苏尔农林牧复合系统 Argan-based Agro-sylvo-pastoral System within the Area of Ait Souab-Ait and Mansour, Morocco	2018
48		埃及 Egypt（1 项）	埃及锡瓦绿洲椰枣生产系统 Dates Production System in Siwa Oasis, Egypt	2016

（续表）

序号	区 域	国 家	系统名称	FAO 批准年份
49	欧洲 Europe（3 国，7 项）	西班牙 Spain（4 项）	西班牙拉阿哈基亚葡萄干生产系统 Málaga Raisin Production System in La Axarquia, Spain	2017
50			西班牙阿尼亚纳海盐生产系统 Salt Production System of Añana, Spain	2017
51			西班牙塞尼亚古橄榄树农业系统 The Agricultural System Ancient Olive Trees Territorio Sénia, Spain	2018
			西班牙瓦伦西亚传统灌溉农业系统 Historical Irrigation System at Horta of Valencia, Spain	2019
52		意大利 Italy（2 项）	意大利阿西西—斯波莱托陡坡橄榄种植系统 Olive Groves of the Slopes between Assisi and Spoleto, Italy	2018
53			意大利索阿维传统葡萄园 Soave Traditional Vineyards, Italy	2018
55		葡萄牙 Portugal（1 项）	葡萄牙巴罗佐农林牧复合系统 Barroso Agro-sylvo-pastral System, Portugal	2018
56	美洲 America（4 国，4 项）	智利 Chile（1 项）	智利智鲁岛屿农业系统 Chiloé Agriculture, Chile	2005
57		秘鲁 Peru（1 项）	秘鲁安第斯高原农业系统 Andean Agriculture, Peru	2005
58		墨西哥 Mexico（1 项）	墨西哥传统架田农作系统 Chinampas Agricultural System of Mexico City, Mexico	2017
59		巴西 Brazil（1 项）	巴西米纳斯吉拉斯埃斯皮尼亚山南部传统农业系统 Traditional Agricultural System in the Southern Espinhaço Range, Minas Gerais, Brazil	2020

中国重要农业文化遗产名录

中国有着悠久灿烂的农耕文化历史，劳动人民在长期的生产活动中创造了种类繁多、特色明显、经济与生态价值高度统一的重要农业文化遗产。至今依然具有重要的历史文化价值和现实意义。农业农村部于 2012 年开展中国重要农业文化遗产发掘与保护工作，旨在加强我国重要农业文化遗产价值的认识，促进遗产地生态保护、文化传承和经济发展。中国重要农业文化遗产是指“人类与其所处环境长期协同发展中，创造并传承至今的独特的农业生产系统，这些系统具有丰富的农业生物多样性、传统知识与技术体系和独特的生态与文化景观等，对我国农业文化传承、农业可持续发展和农业功能拓展具有重要的科学价值和实践意义”。截至 2020 年 4 月，全国共有 5 批 118 项传统农业系统被认定为中国重要农业文化遗产。

The List of China Nationally Important Agricultural Heritage Systems

China has a long and splendid farming cultural history. The labor people in China have created various and unique important agricultural heritage systems, which combine economic and ecological values unanimously. These heritage systems still have important historic and cultural values as well as realistic significance. The Ministry of Agriculture and Rural Affairs of the People's Republic of China have carried out the exploration and conservation of China Nationally Important Agricultural Heritage Systems (China-NIAHS) since 2012. The work aims to strengthen the understanding toward the values of the important agricultural heritage systems in our country and promote the ecological protection, cultural inheritance and economic development of the heritage sites. China-NIAHS are "ingenious agricultural production systems created on the long-term co-adaptation of a rural community/population with its environment and inherited to now, that are rich in biological diversity, traditional knowledge and technologies, remarkable ecological and cultural landscape and are of important scientific and practical relevance to the inheritance, sustainability and multi-functionality of agriculture in China". As of April 2020, a total of 118 traditional agricultural systems of 5 batches have been certified as China-NIAHS.

中国重要农业文化遗产（118 项）

序号	省（区、市）	系统名称	批准年份
1	北京 Beijing （2 项）	北京平谷四座楼麻核桃生产系统 Pinggu Sizuolou Walnut Production System, Beijing Municipality	2015
2		北京京西稻作文化系统 Rice Culture System in the West of Beijing Municipality	2015
3	天津 Tianjin （2 项）	天津滨海崔庄古冬枣园 Cuizhuang Ancient Winter Jujube Gardens, Tianjin Municipality	2014
4		天津津南小站稻种植系统 Xiaozhan Rice Planting System in the South of Tianjin Municipality	2020
5	河北 Hebei （5 项）	河北宣化传统葡萄园 Xuanhua Traditional Vineyards, Hebei Province	2013
6		河北宽城传统板栗栽培系统 Kuancheng Traditional Chestnut Cultivation System, Hebei Province	2014
7		河北涉县旱作梯田系统 Shexian Dryland Terraces System, Hebei Province	2014
8		河北迁西板栗复合栽培系统 Qianxi Chestnut Compound Cultivation System, Hebei Province	2017
9		河北兴隆传统山楂栽培系统 Xinglong Traditional Hawthorn Culture System, Hebei Province	2017
10	山西 Shanxi （1 项）	山西稷山板枣生产系统 Jishan Jujube Production System, Shanxi Province	2017
11	内蒙古 Inner Mongolia （4 项）	内蒙古敖汉旱作农业系统 Aohan Dryland Farming System, Inner Mongolia Autonomous Region	2013
12		内蒙古阿鲁科尔沁草原游牧系统 Arukorqin Grassland Nomadic System, Inner Mongolia Autonomous Region	2014
13		内蒙古伊金霍洛农牧生产系统 Yijinholo Farming and Animal Husbandry Production System, Inner Mongolia Autonomous Region	2017
14		内蒙古乌拉特后旗戈壁红驼牧养系统 Urad Rear Grazing System of Red Camels in Gobi, Inner Mongolia Autonomous Region	2020
15	辽宁 Liaoning （4 项）	辽宁鞍山南果梨栽培系统 Anshan Nanguo Pear Cultivation System, Liaoning Province	2013
16		辽宁宽甸柱参传统栽培体系 Kuandian Shizhu Ginseng Traditional Cultivation System, Liaoning Province	2013
17		辽宁桓仁京租稻栽培系统 Huanren Jingzu Rice Cultivation System, Liaoning Province	2015

（续表）

序号	省（区、市）	系统名称	批准年份
18	辽宁 Liaoning （4 项）	辽宁阜蒙旱作农业系统 Fumeng Dryland Farming System, Liaoning Province	2020
19	吉林 Jilin （3 项）	吉林延边苹果梨栽培系统 Yanbian Apple Pear Cultivation System, Jilin Province	2015
20		吉林柳河山葡萄栽培系统 Liuhe Mountain Grape Cultivation System, Jilin Province	2017
21		吉林九台五官屯贡米栽培系统 Jiutai Wuguantun Tribute Rice Cultivation System, Jilin Province	2017
22	黑龙江 Heilongjiang （2 项）	黑龙江抚远赫哲族鱼文化系统 Fuyuan Fish Culture System of Hezhe Nationality, Heilongjiang Province	2015
23		黑龙江宁安响水稻作文化系统 Ning’an Xiangshui Rice Culture System, Heilongjiang Province	2015
24	江苏 Jiangsu （6 项）	江苏兴化垛田传统农业系统 Xinghua Duotian Traditional Agrosystem, Jiangsu Province	2013
25		江苏泰兴银杏栽培系统 Taixing Ginkgo Cultivation System, Jiangsu Province	2015
26		江苏高邮湖泊湿地农业系统 Gaoyou Lake Wetland Agricultural System, Jiangsu Province	2017
27		江苏无锡阳山水蜜桃栽培系统 Wuxi Yangshan Honey Peach Cultivation System, Jiangsu Province	2017
28		江苏吴中碧螺春茶果复合系统 Wuzhong Biluochun Tea-fruit Compound System, Jiangsu Province	2020
29		江苏宿豫丁嘴金针菜生产系统 Suyu Dingzui Day-lily Production System, Jiangsu Province	2020
30	浙江 Zhejiang （12 项）	浙江青田稻鱼共生系统 Qingtian Rice-fish Culture System, Zhejiang Province	2013
31		浙江绍兴会稽山古香榧群 Shaoxing Kuaijishan Ancient Chinese Torreya, Zhejiang Province	2013
32		浙江杭州西湖龙井茶文化系统 West Lake Dragon Well Tea Culture System, Zhejiang Province	2014
33		浙江湖州桑基鱼塘系统 Huzhou Mulberry Dyke Fish Pond System, Zhejiang Province	2014
34		浙江庆元香菇文化系统 Qingyuan Mushroom Culture System, Zhejiang Province	2014
35		浙江仙居杨梅栽培系统 Xianju Bayberry Cultivation System, Zhejiang Province	2015
36		浙江云和梯田农业系统 Yunhe Terraced Agricultural System, Zhejiang Province	2015

（续表）

序号	省（区、市）	系统名称	批准年份
37	浙江 Zhejiang （12 项）	浙江德清淡水珍珠传统养殖与利用系统 Deqing Freshwater Pearl Traditional Culture and Utilization System, Zhejiang Province	2017
38		浙江宁波黄古林蔺草 - 水稻轮作系统 Ningbo Huanggulin Iris-rice Rotation System, Zhejiang Province	2020
39		浙江安吉竹文化系统 Anji Bamboo Culture System, Zhejiang Province	2020
40		浙江黄岩蜜橘筑墩栽培系统 Huangyan Tangerine Cultivation System Built on Piers, Zhejiang Province	2020
41		浙江开化山泉流水养鱼系统 Kaihua Fish Culture System with Mountain Spring, Zhejiang Province	2020
42	安徽 Anhui （4 项）	安徽寿县芍陂（安丰塘）及灌区农业系统 Shouxian Quebei (Anfengtang) Irrigation Agricultural System, Anhui Province	2015
43		安徽休宁山泉流水养鱼系统 Xiuning Fish Culture System with Mountain Spring, Anhui Province	2015
44		安徽铜陵白姜种植系统 Tongling White Ginger Planting System, Anhui Province	2017
45		安徽黄山太平猴魁茶文化系统 Huangshan Taiping Houkui Tea Culture System, Anhui Province	2017
46	福建 Fujian （4 项）	福建福州茉莉花与茶文化系统 Fuzhou Jasmine and Tea Culture System, Fujian Province	2013
47		福建尤溪联合梯田 Youxi Lianhe Terraces System, Fujian Province	2013
48		福建安溪铁观音茶文化系统 Anxi Tieguanyin Tea Culture System, Fujian Province	2014
49		福建福鼎白茶文化系统 Fuding White Tea Culture System, Fujian Province	2017
50	江西 Jiangxi （6 项）	江西万年稻作文化系统 Wannian Rice Culture System, Jiangxi Province	2013
51		江西崇义客家梯田系统 Chongyi Hakka Terraces System, Jiangxi Province	2014
52		江西南丰蜜橘栽培系统 Nanfeng Tangerine Cultivation System, Jiangxi Province	2017
53		江西广昌传统莲作文化系统 Guangchang Traditional Lotus Culture System, Jiangxi Province	2017
54		江西泰和乌鸡林下养殖系统 Taihe Silky Chicken Culture System Under Forests, Jiangxi Province	2020
55		江西横峰葛根栽培系统 Hengfeng Kudzu Root Cultivation System, Jiangxi Province	2020

（续表）

序号	省（区、市）	系统名称	批准年份
56	山东 Shandong（5 项）	山东夏津黄河故道古桑树群 Traditional Mulberry System in Xiajin's Ancient Yellow River Course, Shandong Province	2014
57		山东枣庄古枣林 Zaozhuang Ancient Jujube Forest, Shandong Province	2015
58		山东乐陵枣林复合系统 Leling Jujube Forest Compound System, Shandong Province	2015
59		山东章丘大葱栽培系统 Zhangqiu Green Chinese Onion Cultivation System, Shandong Province	2017
60		山东泰安汶阳田农作系统 Tai'an Wenyang Field Farming System, Shandong Province	2020
61	河南 Henan（3 项）	河南灵宝川塬古枣林 Lingbao Ancient Jujube Forest in Loess Plateau, Henan Province	2015
62		河南新安传统樱桃种植系统 Xin' an Traditional Cherry Planting System, Henan Province	2017
63		河南嵩县银杏文化系统 Songxian Ginkgo Culture System, Henan Province	2020
64	湖北 Hubei（2 项）	湖北羊楼洞砖茶文化系统 Yangloudong Brick Tea Culture System, Hubei Provinc	2014
65		湖北恩施玉露茶文化系统 Enshi Yulu Tea Culture System, Hubei Province	2015
66	湖南 Hunan（7 项）	湖南新化紫鹊界梯田 Xinhua Ziquejie Terraces System, Hunan Province	2013
67		湖南新晃侗藏红米种植系统 Xinhuang Dong-Tibetan Red Rice Cultivation System, Hunan Province	2014
68		湖南新田三味辣椒种植系统 Xintian Three Flavored Chili Planting System, Hunan Province	2017
69		湖南花垣子腊贡米复合种养系统 Huayuan Zila Tribute Rice Compound Planting and Breeding System, Hunan Province	2017
70		湖南安化黑茶文化系统 Anhua Dark Tea Culture System, Hunan Province	2020
71		湖南保靖黄金寨古茶园与茶文化系统 Baojing Huangjinzhai Ancient Tea Garden and Tea Culture System, Hunan Province	2020
72		湖南永顺油茶林农复合系统 Yongshun Tea-oil Tree Agroforestry System, Hunan Province	2020
73	广东 Guangdong（3 项）	广东潮安凤凰单丛茶文化系统 Chaoan Fenghuang Dancong Tea Culture System, Guangdong Province	2014

（续表）

序号	省（区、市）	系统名称	批准年份
74	广东 Guangdong （3 项）	广东佛山基塘农业系统 Foshan Dyke Pond Agricultural System, Guangdong Province	2020
75		广东岭南荔枝种植系统（增城、东莞） Lingnan Litchi Planting System, Guangdong Province (Zengcheng, Dongguan)	2020
76	广西 Guangxi （4 项）	广西龙胜龙脊梯田系统 Longsheng Longji Terraces System, Guangxi Zhuang Autonomous Region	2014
77		广西隆安壮族“那文化”稻作文化系统 Long’an Zhuang Nationality Rice Culture System of “Na Culture”, Guangxi Province	2015
78		广西恭城月柿栽培系统 Gongcheng Persimmon Cultivation System, Guangxi Province	2017
79		广西横县茉莉花复合栽培系统 Hengxian Jasmine Compound Cultivation System, Guangxi Province	2020
80	海南 Hainan （2 项）	海南海口羊山荔枝种植系统 Haikou Yangshan Litchi Planting System, Hainan Povince	2017
81		海南琼中山兰稻作文化系统 Qiongzhong Shanlan Rice Culture System, Hainan Province	2017
82	重庆 Chongqing （3 项）	重庆石柱黄连生产系统 Shizhu Coptis Production System, Chongqing Province	2017
83		重庆大足黑山羊传统养殖系统 Big-foot Black Goat Traditional Culture System, Chongqing Province	2020
84		重庆万州红桔栽培系统 Wanzhou Red Orange Cultivation System, Chongqing Province	2020
85	四川 Sichuan （8 项）	四川江油辛夷花传统栽培体系 Jiangyou Magnolia Flower Traditional Cultivation System, Sichuan Province	2014
86		四川苍溪雪梨栽培系统 Cangxi Pear Cultivation System, Sichuan Province	2015
87		四川美姑苦荞栽培系统 Meigu Buckwheat Cultivation System, Sichuan Povince	2015
88		四川盐亭嫘祖蚕桑生产系统 Yanting Leizu Sericulture Production System, Sichuan Province	2017
89		四川名山蒙顶山茶文化系统 Mingshan Mengding Mountain Tea Culture System, Sichuan Province	2017
90		四川郫都林盘农耕文化系统 Pidu Bamboo Forest and Farming Culture System, Sichuan Province	2020
91		四川宜宾竹文化系统 Yibin Bamboo Culture System, Sichuan Province	2020

（续表）

序号	省（区、市）	系统名称	批准年份
92	四川 Sichuan （8 项）	四川石渠扎溪卡游牧系统 Shiqu Zhaxika Nomadic System, Sichuan Province	2020
93	贵州 Guizhou （4 项）	贵州从江侗乡稻鱼鸭系统 Congjiang Dong' s Rice-fish-duck System, Guizhou Province	2013
94		贵州花溪古茶树与茶文化系统 Huaxi Ancient Tea Trees and Tea Culture System, Guizhou Province	2015
95		贵州锦屏杉木传统种植与管理系统 Jinping Chinese Fir Traditional Planting and Management System, Guizhou Province	2020
96		贵州安顺屯堡农业系统 Anshun Statioin Troop Agricultural System, Guizhou Province	2020
97	云南 Yunnan （7 项）	云南红河哈尼稻作梯田系统 Honghe Hani Rice Terrace System, Yunnan Province	2013
98		云南普洱古茶园与茶文化系统 Yunnan Pu' er Traditioanl Tea Garden and Tea Culture System	2013
99		云南漾濞核桃 - 作物复合系统 Yangbi Walnut and Crop Composite System, Yunnan Province	2013
100		云南广南八宝稻作生态系统 Guangnan Babao Rice Ecological Cultivation System, Yunnan Province	2014
101		云南剑川稻麦复种系统 Jianchuan Rice-wheat Multiple Cropping System, Yunnan Province	2014
102		云南双江勐库古茶园与茶文化系统 Shuangjiang Mengku Ancient Tea Garden and Tea Culture System, Yunnan Province	2014
103		云南腾冲槟榔江水牛养殖系统 Tengchong Breeding System of Water Buffalo in Betel River, Yunnan Province	2017
104	陕西 Shaanxi （4 项）	陕西佳县古枣园 Jiaxian Traditional Chinese Date Gardens, Shaanxi Province	2013
105		陕西凤县大红袍花椒栽培系统 Fengxian Dahongpao Pepper Cultivation System, Shaanxi Province	2017
106		陕西蓝田大杏种植系统 Lantian Apricot Planting System, Shaanxi Province	2017
107		陕西临潼石榴种植系统 Lintong Pomegranate Planting System, Shaanxi Province	2020
108	甘肃 Gansu （4 项）	甘肃皋兰什川古梨园 Shichuan Traditional Pear Gardens, Gansu Province	2013

（续表）

序号	省（区、市）	系统名称	批准年份
109	甘肃 Gansu （4 项）	甘肃迭部扎尕那农林牧复合系统 Diebu Zhagana Agriculture-Forest-Animal Husbandry Compound System, Gansu Province	2013
110		甘肃岷县当归种植系统 Minxian Angelica Sinensis Cropping System, Gansu Province	2014
111		甘肃永登苦水玫瑰农作系统 Yongdeng Kushui Rose Farming System, Gansu Province	2015
112	新疆 Xinjiang （4 项）	新疆吐鲁番坎儿井农业系统 Turfan Karez Agricultural System, Xinjiang Uygur Autonomous region	2013
113		新疆哈密市哈密瓜栽培与贡瓜文化系统 Hami Melon Cultivation and Tribute Culture System, Xinjiang Uygur Autonomous region	2014
114		新疆奇台旱作农业系统 Qitai Dryland Farming System, Xinjiang Uygur Autonomous region	2015
115		新疆伊犁察布查尔布哈农业系统 Ili Chabuchar Buha Agricultural System, Xinjiang Uygur Autonomous region	2017
116	宁夏 Ningxia （3 项）	宁夏灵武长枣种植系统 Lingwu Long Jujube Planting System, Ningxia Hui Autonomous Region	2014
117		宁夏中宁枸杞种植系统 Zhongning Lycium Barbarum Planting System, Ningxia Hui Autonomous Region	2015
118		宁夏盐池滩羊养殖系统 Yanchi Tan Sheep Breeding System, Ningxia Hui Autonomous Region	2017